ALIVE IN THIS WORLD

ALIVE
IN THIS
W★RLD

A Memoir

*Tracking Light Through the
Wilderness of Grief*

LYSSA BLACK FASSETT

DARBYTREE
PUBLISHING

GROTON, MA, USA

Cataloging-in-Publication Data is on file with the Library of Congress
Paperback ISBN: 978-0-578-32672-6

Lyrics from "Stand," by the Kennedys, reprinted by permission.

Design by Christina Thiele, CreateForGood
Editorial production by kn literary

Printed in the United States of America
1 3 5 7 9 10 8 6 4 2

DarbyTree Publishing
Groton, Massachusetts

For Darby, my North Star,
whose light continues to shine

CONTENTS

INTRODUCTION

A PORTAL

t's a cool spring day in the Northeast as I look out my office window and watch the cardinal who has taken to perching on the cable wire across the street, a tiny blaze of crimson through the pine boughs, full-blown forsythia, and trees not yet budded out. My cat, Lotus, waits patiently for me to open the door so she can enter and curl up on the windowsill beside my desk. The sounds of Native American flutes and drums from an iPod weave in and out of my awareness as I stare at my computer screen, digging a little deeper for the right constellation of words. And a small candle flickers in front of a picture of my son, Darby, in a cow outfit he gladly agreed to drape over his six-foot frame as a promo gimmick outside the restaurant where he worked before heading to college. That ironic smile and sparkle in his eyes captivate me, and an ocean of love wells up as the flute music fills the room. I close my eyes—a tangle of emotions overtaking me: *loving you, missing you, but feeling you here with me, all in the same moment.* An unimaginable crack in my universe has reimagined itself as an infinitely expanded space where life, death, and time itself take on new meaning. Where am I on this day?

I think about the trajectory of my life in the ten years since Darby died and see in my mind's eye a long journey into the frightful woods, but, as with the ancient fairy tales, it's not a journey through time and space, but the parting of a curtain as my "spiritual eyes" adjust to the light. In her book *The Miracle of Death*, Betty Kovacs, a professor of literature, myth, and symbolic language, says that "the core experience of the book is the stark reality of the death of all those I loved most in the world. For it was death—that fundamental mystery of life—that opened me to a vast and loving universe."

One day, five years after my son's death, I realized in a sudden flash of understanding how grief functions, what it is *for*. Grief is a teacher hiding in a whirlwind of terror and chaos. Grief tore me apart, then opened my heart. Its waves both crushed and liberated me as they moved in and out. I woke up to moments of clarity around this new reality of my son's physical absence and my own spiritual growth. Over and over again, an open heart created a portal into the next wave of the journey. It is *all* about expansion of the heart, and despite the machinations of the ego-mind, the roller coaster of extreme emotions and the difficult work of realization, the process itself could not be simpler. This flash of understanding didn't happen in a vacuum, however; and that is a critical part of my story. In addition to my husband, family, friends, and a myriad of others who offered healing, each in their own way, I was serendipitously led to a high-spirited guide and "energy tracker" who lit my way out of the woods by encouraging me to find the light within myself, to learn to play with this new world revealing itself, to feel joy again.

Do we really move on from deep loss? Or can we surrender and allow our beloved's absence to come to us and show us its face, slowly, quietly, gracefully, until "reality" is radically transformed? What was lost is found and was, in fact, always there. Loss and presence, living within us in perfect balance. I wrote this book based on the journal I kept as I moved through overwhelming grief and loneliness after my son overdosed on heroin at the age of twenty-two. If grief is anything, it is profoundly lonely, no matter how many people love and surround you, and so I wrote to save myself. And then, after my confusion cleared, to pay it forward in gratitude for others' stories that helped me believe in the hope of healing and return to wholeness that I knew in my bones was possible.

After all, what has this journey been about? Honoring my beloved son by opening myself as wide as I can to the spectacular beauty and mystery of the universe we all inhabit, and to love him in everything I do. This is the story of a grieving mother, a lost son, and a mentor who helped me find him and so much more in a series of adventure-sessions that changed everything.

———

CHAPTER ONE

THE END OF TIME

MAY 7, 2008

For grief to do its work, to cleanse and to purify,
I had to grow a new body to contain it. For my heart
to reemerge into the light of the world, I had to wrestle
unimaginable pain and choose another horizon.

The night is getting on, and my collection of small irritations is growing. I tap my fingers on the kitchen table as I stare at the computer, my mind wandering as I resist Googling one more company for job openings I don't really want. I hardly ever hear the kitchen clock ticking as the minutes go by, but I hear it now. It's almost 11:00. My husband, Dan, said something earlier that pissed me off; I don't remember exactly what it was, but I'm still pissed. And my mother is here. She's been visiting us for the past few weeks, up from Boston where she lives with my brother who looks after her now. She is back home after twenty years of living in Hawaii, a dream she had nurtured for many years but had to abandon because her funds had run out. She brought back a vague resentment about finding herself in this position, reflecting a long-standing dissatisfaction with much of her life. I'm glad she's safely back home and grateful to my brother for taking her in, but her attitude, triggering my own negativity, eventually always gets to me. I'm happy she got to talk to Darby when he called this afternoon—it's a rare occurrence when all three of us are here to touch base with our boy. But I want my space back.

My phone rings, pulling me away from my musing about my mother and my space. It's Darby. *Hmm,* I wonder, *we just talked to you this afternoon.*

"Hi, Darb! What—" An unfamiliar man's voice cuts in, identifies himself as a paramedic calling from Northampton where Darby lives.

"We're performing critical life-saving procedures on your son." That's all I hear. Full stop. I don't understand—what is he saying? His words ricochet inside my head, shock beginning to create chaos in my brain while I remain frozen in place. I have to ask him to repeat himself. He asks me questions. "Does your son have any medical conditions? Is he taking any medications?" I can hear myself talking so I know that words are coming out of my mouth, but a part of me is coming apart, and I start falling. I double over, not comprehending what is happening, what is going on with my son, or whether he is even still alive. I must be making sounds of some sort because Dan comes running into to the kitchen, looking distressed. I hear my mother shouting, "What is going on?" I clutch the phone as if it has fused with my fist, straighten into a standing position as my mother appears. I see the fear on her face, and I try to calm her. I tell Dan that the two of us need to leave for Northampton *now.*

The drive along the dark, lonely highway to Cooley Dickinson Hospital is two hours of electric paralysis. We clutch each other, not knowing what to think or feel or be—*what the fuck is happening?* Our son is away at college; we each talked to him just this afternoon—nothing remarkable, just normal chatter, laughter tumbling over the surface of shared love that was simply a given.

We walk through the hospital doors, fear pounding in our heads, into the hush of a beige, antiseptic universe to face a reality where everything has altered in an instant. We are ushered into a small, unoccupied room. It's too quiet. Where is the doctor? Where is my son? The doctor finally comes into the room, calmly sits down on the chair in front of us. No expression on her face that I can recognize through the thundering river of horror coursing through my body. I hear her words, but they won't sink into my brain: *heroin overdose.* Dan calmly asks what is now obvious to us both, "He passed away?" A nod and a yes.

What's going on? What do you mean? *Heroin?* Everything in me is shutting down. We didn't know. We never had a chance.

We're finished here. Finished with doctors. I stumble through the hospital parking lot. I'm shouting at Dan and the night sky, "What do we do now?" Then, I'm staring out the car window at nothing as we travel the few miles to Darby's house. Dan combs our son's room for incriminating evidence that might have harmed our boy, a parental instinct still very much alive. I don't think I'm speaking while Dan drives us back home, but I can't be sure. He's making the calls—to my older brother, who he had asked earlier to come stay with our mother, to a few other family members, who are waiting to hear the outcome of our rush to the hospital. The shock has wrapped me in a blanket of eerie stillness; eyes open, brain comatose.

Dan and I had both known something was off-balance with Darby lately—Dan more willing to acknowledge it than I had been. He'd looked like hell when he was home for Christmas, and he hadn't returned our phone calls that winter as he usually had. In hindsight, there were many small signs, each of them easily explained away, especially by someone, like me, who was in denial. We knew he was no stranger to risky behavior, including drugs. But because he wasn't living with us, and he loved us, we were blindsided. We knew nothing of his addiction, and that's the way he would have wanted it. He would have kept the trouble he was in to himself.

We arrive home in the early dawn light, its otherworldly, liminal quality matching our shaken reality. My brother, Dana, standing in the driveway, embraces me with a wordless hug. Inside, I collapse on the sofa beside my mother, who puts her arm around me and strokes my hand. The fatigue and shock are taking their toll on us. Dan and I go to bed and wail in each other's arms.

How do I locate myself now?

—

I have no weight. No definition. I hear familiar voices in the living room but cannot decipher anything they say. I might float away or sink or just cease to exist, but what does this mean? I cannot make meaning. I flail here, unprotected within a violent storm of unrelenting emotional, physical, and mental anguish. Panic, shock, hopelessness, terror—how am I still breathing? I crawl through every second, minute, hour, day, telling myself, *If I can just get through the coming week, I will be that much farther away from ground zero, and maybe I can find a speck of hope in that.*

My old life is gone. Every moment is unbearably long, yet oddly insubstantial. I cannot conjure the words to tell. Just this: a gravitational pull that seems to swallow my every thought, every word, every breath as it catches in my clenching gut, like contractions, ones that won't usher in new life. Eyeing a loaf of bread a friend has brought over, I think, *I must eat,* but food is like sawdust in my mouth: My throat contracts; I can't swallow. Books, movies, TV? Bled of all their juice, they exist in an unfamiliar, flat dimension, too pale to penetrate the space I now inhabit, diversion *verboten.* The only reliefs left to me are hot baths—an elemental medium that seems to calm me—and sleep, which exacts a heavy price because, of course, I have to wake up tomorrow.

Day comes, and I sleepwalk through the house, surrounded by the ghostly trail of a life that has vanished without warning. Our friend Ray knocks on the door but doesn't come in. He offers soup and a gentle presence. He remarks that driving up our road doesn't even seem the same anymore. I blink in the early afternoon sun; I am here and not here. Part of me has gone away.

Night comes again. I lie prostrate on my bed, my body crushed into the sheets, and petition the universe for release from this suffering. I ask for mercy. I ask for the light of understanding. I beg for the strength to surrender utterly to the whole of this experience, wherever it takes me, because if I know anything now, it is that I cannot live like this.

I steal through the shadowy, sleeping house a week after my son left the world. The bright moon and stars draw me out the front door. I sink down on the wooden steps, keeping the porch door open a crack to hear better—and avoid—anyone who might awaken and come looking for me. I search the night sky for a trace, a whisper, of clarity. And then, the spinning in my mind abruptly subsides. Grief relaxes its suffocating grip, and I am released for the time it takes to see what's right in front of me. In this supercharged universe, the cats emerge from darkness and brush against my legs before disappearing back into the shadows, while my family sleeps inside the home I have brought up my son in, worked in, lived in, for the past twenty-five years. The night wraps its arms around me. I am held, I am blessed, and everything is completely out of my control. The how-why-what stream of thought that holds my mind captive on any given day falls like dust at my feet in this moment. I shiver and open my entire consciousness to the indigo sky. What channels up from the deep, through the dust and stasis, tells me with spotless certainty that *I will get to the bottom of this; I will find my son, and I will heal.*

Find him. Find my dead son. If there is a skeptical thought forming itself around this awareness, it crumbles without resistance. No, my mind is not grasping for a comforting idea, because comfort is lost to me now. This knowledge has the ancient weight of a seed planted in the desert that waits for years for the right conditions to allow it to bloom.

—

CHAPTER TWO

BLOWN APART

MAY 13, 2008

First Week

Pulled from the blessed relief of deep, dreamless sleep by Dan's gentle but urgent coaxing to arise and begin the difficult arc of this day, my body tenses as my eyes adjust to the early light. Our son has been lying in a hospital morgue—*no, not possible*—for over a week, and this is the day. Our itinerary: We will drive to the morgue in Holyoke to pick up our son's body. We will meet his cousins in nearby Northampton, and afterward, we will make a stop near the house he shared with roommates just outside Northampton for an informal wake. Finally, we will travel across the border to Vermont and the crematorium serving the western Massachusetts and southern Vermont area. But I can't say these words out loud; I can barely think these words.

Just last night, Darby's cousins were here, bringing us supper, holding us up in the buoyant strength of their young lives—where Darby should be. *No, don't say that!* Dan and I, however flawed, always had our arms out to catch him. Meetings with his teachers when his rebelliousness at the tediousness and restrictiveness of school got him in trouble. Dan driving hours to Vermont with a spare car key when Darby lost his on a ski slope. Encouragement that he was capable of achieving his dreams. Everyday reassurance that he was loved and protected. This time, he had gone too far, too fast to be caught— beyond our outstretched arms that we had naively believed could be enough. We hadn't been able to help our boy in those last moments, but strange as it seems, we could care for him now. We understood this was the only option available for us.

"This is all we need," Dan said, referencing the simple box meant for our son.

I heard this cut-and-dried declaration as he talked on the phone to the funeral home, and it circled my brain like a bird in flight unable to find a place to land. My nieces and nephews had arrived—my surrogate kids. My ninety-year-old mother sat silently on the couch, her heart breaking, while we opened cartons of food. I thought of my father, a grandfather Darby hadn't known, either as a physical presence or in the family stories we tell. He left me suddenly, too, with no chance to say good-bye, or ask why, or to say, "I love you." I was a little girl when my father walked out of our house and disappeared from my life. I'd kept that loss locked inside for years, but he was here tonight.

We hesitated, sometimes struggling to find language that made sense in this strange space. Dan shared a story he'd heard from Darby's friends: When he died, Darby wanted to be cremated and stuffed inside a giant taco and fed to the wolves. Against all odds, laughter spilled out into the house. This tidbit of Darby lore that I hadn't known became precious to me.

Dan brought in the box, which had been positioned in the bed of his pickup, and as if we had planned it, we grabbed markers, colored pencils, watercolors, and went to work. Gigantic yellow tacos, cartoon wolves, poems of love, and messages of grief and safe passage for Darby bloomed inside and outside this plain piece of cardboard that would take Darby home. My mother, Marnie to her grandchildren, observed it all with a solemn silence and lent a profound dimension to what unfolded simply by her presence. Death is an initiation.

Our ancestors knew this; what we found ourselves doing on this night would be well known to them.

But on this new morning, Dan and I are alone, my mother back at her home, our nieces and nephews meeting us in Northampton later in the day. There seems to be nothing outside this house—no life, no motion, no reality. The morning light is the only substance penetrating my mind-fog. It is cruel and cutting in its soft luminescence. All this is light and life, yet our son is dead. I don't know how I will make it through this day.

I collect the printouts of official regulations we have researched that cover our rights as citizens to pick up our son's body. Yes, state law allows us to transport him ourselves. No, bodies do not decompose quickly. No, it is not required that funeral homes control this process. Yes, we have more legal control over caring for our loved ones than most people are aware of. We have done our homework with the help of our friends, church community, and Google. These thoughts both horrify me and help me put one foot in front of the other.

Let me be clear: Dan steers this train today. I am incapable, in another world, just barely touching this one. Dan's devastation plays out today in hyperattention—lucky for me. None of this seems real, but it must be done. Thank you, thank you; I can't begin to tell you how grateful I am to you, that I can remain in this stasis for a while—don't shake the container; it might shatter into uncountable pieces.

Yet Dan has every reason to feel this tragedy as an especially cruel and punishing blow. Darby had an older half-sister, Wreath Rose, who died in a car crash eleven years before at the age of twenty-five. Dan had been a young father who made it a priority to keep Wreath in his life when his marriage fell apart. Smart, funny, kind, and creative, she was always ahead of the curve with the social trends of the day, but also always had time for her little brother when she came to visit in the summers. At her funeral in Colorado, where she lived with the man she had married just five months before, Darby stood by his sister's casket and showed off the University of Colorado Buffs T-shirt she had given him when she was a student. I watched as he dropped a woven friendship bracelet into the casket and grieved in his own way for their lost relationship. Dan told me later, "I found a way to integrate my grief with my spirituality. I never in a million years thought I'd have to again."

Everything about this day is wrong. But we drive westward to Holyoke, to the morgue, to get our son. I hear Dan on the phone arguing, advocating, asking, explaining what we are attempting to do—simple to us but foreign to the faceless officials mediating our caring for our son. Agitation fills the car as he tangles with officials who apparently have no experience with what we want to do—handle death on our own terms. It is just assumed that we can't pick up our son's body. They worry about legalities and liability, but we have done our homework well. *Will it matter?* I wonder. He must be talking to the medical examiner. *You can't pick up the body, health reasons, illegal to transport a body across state lines, you need a lawyer, go away.* The world outside the windshield catches my eye; I can't help it. The hazy cloudiness of the day has gone. Now, sun, spring wildflowers, and light everywhere. Green grass and luminous daylight surrounding the morgue as we make our way around the bend into the parking lot. I won't get out of the car. I can't talk to anyone. This sharp beauty drags me down until I have to close my eyes.

Dan comes back to the car; we are told we need to go to Northampton to fill out a transportation permit. By this time, an angel by the name of Jim Curley, the owner of the crematorium in Vermont, has become our greatest advocate. He is, in effect, our legal proxy. Without his guidance via phone through the thicket of interstate law, protocol, and official resistance to the simple act of collecting our son and caring for him in our own way, we cannot do what we came here to do.

The Business of Death

Darby's cousins are waiting for us. The knot of tension in my solar plexus tightens as we get closer. *He should be here.* The road to Northampton, car noise, sun burning my arms, sharp edges—I narrow my gaze to a focus that won't kill me. Not Whole Foods, where he worked between classes. Not Bay Street in Hadley where he lived, the same road where I lived as a student decades before. Not over there, on the railroad bridge, where he rode his bicycle before his license was returned, or that right turn where the paramedics rushed him to the hospital. Dan can't help me. I can't help him.

We park behind the town hall, a small, close space nestled below busy Main Street. Inside, the clerk finally gives us the form we need after a prolonged, dubious questioning. *Why the fuck are you torturing us like this?* I want to throw it in her pinched face, because I hate her; I despise every fucking thing about this fucking, fucking day. I run out the door, leaving Dan to deal with her. *Please, Darby, where are you? Please, please . . .* Dan finds me, tries to comfort me while holding a piece of paper that allows him to carry his son out in a box, to his truck bed, to a crematorium, to swallow him up as if he had never been here. I have no comfort to give. I am a complete piece of shit. *I should have saved him I cannot live without him I am losing my mind right here on the sidewalk people staring at me judging me assholes all.*

We walk to Thornes Marketplace on Main Street to find a place to sit and fill out the form. *Where is he?* In between everything I see here, inside the stores and cafes, the corridors, around the corners, is a thin layer of pale light where I perceive his absence, which is something rather than nothing. We find a bench near the vegetarian restaurant where we met up with Darby not so long ago. I write his name, his date of birth—words and more words that must be laid down with an exactitude that refocuses me after my meltdown at the town hall. But someone passes by, someone laughs, and the second I look away, the pale light captures me. I peer intently into it but can't see him. He's gone. But *here*, everywhere here. Anxiety grips me: Have I filled out this form correctly? I don't know. I don't know anything.

Embracing Our Son

Form in hand, we drive back to the morgue in Holyoke, and Dan backs the truck into a parking space near the building's entrance. I stare straight ahead. I tell him I cannot come in with him. He hugs me and gets out of the truck to get our son. All is quiet, still, as if a numbing balm has taken over the heavy work of grief for this moment. I reach for the door and walk out into penetrating sunlight. In the field surrounding the sprawling brick building, I see a picnic bench. No one there; it is mine for a time. The peaceful blue gentleness of the May sky, bright dandelions sprouting up all around me, new green leaves on trees catching the breeze. As the earth wakes up with tenderness this spring, I sit, barely moving, collapsing inside. The absolute vastness of Darby's absence on the planet—my heart is filled with him. My eyes are shocked by what they see here.

Back inside the truck, my mind goes blank, overloading again with the emotions of the day. At first, I hear them—men helping Dan haul the box that contains our son into the truck bed. Dan calls me outside, and I turn to face him once I can no longer hear their conversation. I walk up the short path to join him and the medical examiner, who, earlier in the day, had thrown cold water on our plan, but now wishes us well and hugs us, tears in her eyes, "after all that has transpired" in our journey. The sun is sinking low even though our day isn't even close to being over. We need to make our way to the town of Hadley, where Darby lived as a student and where his friends are gathering now, and then to the crematorium a good hour away in Vermont. I'm back in the passenger seat, imagining Darby right behind me, separated by the cab's window. I remember a trip to Prince Edward Island when he was little, Dan at the wheel, and the two of us snuggled up in blankets in the back of a previous family truck, giggling as we made up tales of a leprechaun Olympics to see us home. Thankfully, Dan interrupts this mental road to hell to tell me that the two morgue attendants were deeply touched by what we were doing and hoped they might make the same decision someday. I am grateful for their support. I am grateful to the medical examiner for her compassion. I am immeasurably grateful to Dan for his love and caring for me. We are all, after all, in this life together. We wend our way down the crooked road, the anxiety of officialdom subsided, the deep breath of the ending chapter of this day coming on.

Ceremony

I begin to feel the pieces of this day lose their jagged edge, and sorrow envelops everything like bitter honey. I am waterlogged by it. I move in slow motion with the enormity of what this day means. We drive down the long, bucolic arc of Bay Road until we come to rest at the home of one his dear friends in Hadley, a stone's throw from the house where Darby lived with his roommates, until the fall, when he and his girlfriend planned to move in together for his last year at UMass. His friends are here: some schoolmates, some work colleagues, some from his childhood network of Unitarian youth group companions. His cousins, following Dan and me in their car from our meeting place in

Northampton, join the widening circle on the front lawn while Dan and helpers open the truck and ease Darby out of it, lowering him onto the small deck of the house. I watch from a distance.

Dan unzips the body bag. As he leans over Darby and cuts a piece of his hair and murmurs something so gently I can't make it out, the gathering of those who love Darby coalesce around him in semi-silence. His high school sweetheart sobs in the arms of her boyfriend, who is also one of our son's earliest and dearest friends. Everyone in turn connects with their young friend, in verse, song, heartfelt words of grief and disbelief. I move to the periphery, unable in that moment to look at his beautiful pale face, his hidden blue eyes, his short, sandy hair brushing his ears, his body lying so still; I am such a coward. But I can't just leave him there. I turn toward him and see, and my love rushes through my body as if there were no body there and completely engulfs my child.

Cremation

With help, Dan gingerly places our son back in the truck, and with his cousins, we prepare to leave for the last station of this journey. We each say good-bye to Darby's friends with long, silent hugs as day transitions to night, continuing on what feels like an endless road since morning. I check the rearview mirror and see them following behind, a solemn caravan doing the only thing it *can* do—continue. We finally come to rest in Vermont, at the crematorium we have chosen. Jim, the owner/operator whose advocacy helped us keep our sanity on the long drive up here, is a bear of a man, compassion shining from his eyes as he greets us with hugs. He opens the doors for us, into the large, converted barn where the inner workings of a scenario I never imagined I'd find myself in lay exposed to our weary eyes. This all begins to feel like dreamland, where everything floats and everything sinks; it's all the same to me. My son is in a box in a building where his sweet body will disappear from the Earth. The seven of us stand around him in a circle and offer our love to him, wish him a good journey, until our words end and there is only holy silence.

It begins. The machinery cranks up, and Dan and I touch Darby's head under the cover of the thin cardboard box. We then place our hands over the "On" button, gently push down, and we let him go. I leave my body too.

I watch myself as I push that button and wonder how I could possibly do this. Am I horrified at my willingness to do such an unthinkable thing? Proud that I am able to show up for my son until the literal end?

Jim kindly invites all of us to his farmhouse, just up the road from the crematorium, while we wait the four hours it will take. His wife, Ellen, comes home from work with a smile and an offer of grilled-cheese sandwiches. I haven't thought about food, but Ellen's motherly kindness sparks a flame of gratitude in me that spreads outward and all around me to everything I observe. The warm country kitchen opens up to a modern living space where the land—gardens, mowed land, sheds, and lovely old trees—stretches out beyond the large bay windows. A professional telescope stands ready for observing the night sky unobstructed by city lights.

Lamps bathe the house in a muted glow as dusk comes on. I slump back on a comfortable leather chair near the kitchen, swallowing warm cheese and crusty bread as I try to locate myself in the whirlwind of this day. Tears rim my eyes but don't fall. All is over and all has just begun. I look up and notice my nephew, Mark, walking over with a laptop. He sets it on a small table in front of the semicircle of chairs in which we are resting and begins a slideshow. These are Darby's photos, taken around Amherst and on his travels during the enthusiastic days of his career goal of being a backpack journalist—each image disappearing into another. "Thank you, Mark," I whisper.

Night falls. The slide show goes on in an endless loop as we take note of the darkening sky and turn inward to our own thoughts. We watch from the windows as Jim comes into sight, climbing up the hill from the crematory. Cremation is a long process, and when he comes into the house, he suggests starting a bonfire out in the field for us. *Yes, yes.* He builds the fire slowly, mindfully, lovingly. We follow him out into the yard, the cool spring night surrounding us as we throw fallen branches into the flames. I look out past the dark field and stars overhead, my thoughts traveling down the hill, where the work of "ashes to ashes" is still in progress. I can't think; I can only stare into this wilderness and stand in awe of it.

Dan and I hug; no words. The fire grows, we weave around it, and songs come, stories come out of the shadow. Darby stories, from shared cousin-time of years ago or maybe just last Christmas. Quiet laughter ripples through the night of tears and gives way to songs we all know from our shared Unitarian church background. I sit on one of the wooden chairs positioned on the periphery of the blazing fire that sends up flares to the dark sky. Ellen puts an arm around me, and I sink into a place so deep and otherworldly that tears can't even find me.

I love you, Darby; I love you, I love you, and that is all there is in this moment.

Love, death, family, starry night, and inhalation/exhalation of communal breath—there is no separation. The only thought available to me is, *This is what holiness is; this is sacred ground.*

CHAPTER THREE

SURVIVAL

MAY-JUNE 2008

I saw you flying over Acadia this morning,
That happy, joyous smile on your face. Arms stretched out
to infinity, soaring with the wild ocean breeze
above the Rocks.
I wanted to catch you, to go with you,
but it was good to see you happy
and free.

—Vision-Dream from Darby

Drifting

This is how I live now. I lie on my bed, summer sun filtering in through the half-open blinds. Morning? Early afternoon? I don't know, don't know. People outside, cleaning our yard, carrying brush away, pulling down the rickety tree house Dan built for Darby when he was a little boy. Friends from our church community, gathered here to help out a grieving, devastated family, but I am so far away. I think there may be people in my living room; my mother, brothers, neighbors? But I drift here on my bed, above my bed, my mind everywhere and nowhere, and I can't go out to greet them, to thank them, because I no longer exist. My thoughts, my feelings, my bodily functions, my self-awareness are a jumble of electrical impulses flowing all over the place, but no longer contained in "I." I can't imagine what this means; I have no power, no will to create meaning, and so I drift.

I wake each morning and, within seconds of full consciousness, feel my gut roil. A memory-image, like a beautiful, deadly snake, rises up. My son, swinging in a hammock under the immense night sky of Prince Edward Island on a solo getaway a few weeks before he set off to UMass Amherst. Bored with the entire concept of high school and pushing the boundaries in both creative and dangerous ways, he barely got out with a passing grade. His road trip to this place we all loved and visited many times together was a celebration of the hard work and focus he put into community college when at last the light switched on.

He brought his guitar with him to keep himself company, an acoustic his dad bought for him to add to his collection, which included a robin's-egg blue Fender Stratocaster, the same model his hero, Kurt Cobain, played. The thread of music wove the three of us together from the start—we took Darby to his first concert, the Newport Folk Festival, when he was three weeks old. Dan and I still play in a band that started years ago in our friend's kitchen. And a young Darby picked the guitar up with very little instruction, the music seeming to move through him effortlessly.

One night, he called as he was lying beneath the amazing field of stars at Green Park Provincial Park, reading a book by Jon Krakauer I recommended to him and that we both loved, *Into Thin Air*. He told me how beautiful and peaceful it was, how much he loved it there, listening to the little waves lap the shore of PEI's red-clay sand, the dark sky vivid with stars in the absence of city lights. We talked for a while in that easy rhythm of familiarity, ending, as always, with "Love you." In the impossible light of this new morning, I see his long, slim body stretched out in the hammock he'd packed, swaddled in his hoodie, book resting on his chest as he scans the heavens, the vast night enveloping him like a warm blanket, and I cannot bear it.

Waterfall

I am drawn like a starving person to water. Long, steaming, aromatic baths that seem to be the only environment, except dreamless sleep, that soothes me. It is miraculous. I step into the bathtub, sometimes many times during a single day, and the roiling goes away. I don't meditate, I don't journal, I don't hope—I am rocked like a baby to a state of some kind of equilibrium, and I don't know why or how. I lie in a state of suspended animation as my body disappears and my mind lets go of everything it has gripped so tightly. Dan, grieving himself, is glad for any relief I find; he's at his wit's end, trying to find ways of bringing me back.

He drags me to work with him at our friend Lee's house, a 200-year-old farmhouse with an enchanting waterfall, while he finishes a carpentry job for her. Lee and I don't see each other often, but I've always cherished our wry, soulful excavations of the human spirit. She's a saving light for me today. She embraces us both; strong, wordless hugs, then Dan begins his day's work in another room, and Lee and I sit at her sunny kitchen table with mugs of coffee, golden retrievers at our feet, birds chattering at the feeders on the other side of the big bay window. *Why did Darby leave us?* That question, no answers, much heavy digging into the spiritual realm. But the fatigue that comes to me now like slow-moving fog overtakes me. I thank her and leave the kitchen, catching a peek of Dan focused on the wall he is painting, and my heart breaks for him too. It would be better if I could lose myself in work—everyone tells me so. I no longer have a job to go to, having been laid off six months ago, and now, I can't seem to focus on anything; all thought and emotion caught in this inner turbulence. But I know that Dan's suffering surrounds him, and I feel too insubstantial to help. I tell him I need to lie down, and I leave the house, following the small wooden footbridge connecting Lee's flowering backyard to the waterfall just beyond.

I've stood here many times before. I've watched the stream that flows over an old embankment, creating a small waterfall, and the wildlife that finds a home here. I have helped Lee weed her flowerbeds and sat with her in lawn chairs, talking about the books we've read and the spiritual experiences we've had. Right now, I am simply outside, where the elementals live. I look for a place to rest and decide the patch of hard ground between a tangle of tree roots near the stream's bank will do. I lie down, the water devas comforting my shattered heart as I drift to a shadowy land between sleep and wakefulness. I listen awhile under the incongruous summer sun illuminating everything in its path with different shades and depths of gold. The sun shines regardless of my grief, and my mind is unable to make meaning from this. So be it. But thoughts come—from the streaming water, from the birds, from the drifting clouds. I think of the waterfall in front of me. It tells me it is the bloodstream of the world. But this world—the material world—is the hard one. We come in kicking and screaming and go out the same way.

When I looked in your eyes these past several years, I saw a troubled soul and tried to help you the best I could. Reassure you, love you, guide you. And I am so very afraid that if I let go of you, I will lose you— what can this possibly mean in the face of your absence?

The world has shifted, my navigational system useless in this new landscape. But these words and thoughts just glide across the surface of the landslide moving underneath. Where do I go? What do I do? What am I supposed to be now? The center of my being, where Darby is but isn't. How can this be? I have finally reached a place in my life where there is nowhere to hide: it is the freedom of the mad and the broken.

I observe the great blue heron I have seen here before, perched on a log half-submerged in the pond just beyond the place where the water falls, who watches over me now.

You left a feather on Lee's doorstep last night. She said it was for me, a gift from you, a gift from Darby. Thank you for showing up. Thank you for your witness.

Wandering

The heron feather has joined its brethren in the clay feather jar, standing tall among the generations of feathers found on walks around the country, all magical and meaningful. I drip onto the wood floor below, emerging from yet another long bath in the middle of the day, at my bedroom window, alone. My neurotic list-making can't find traction in this space, and through a quirky twist of fate, the universe seems to have set me up to take this dive into the unknown with few distractions. Like a job. Laid off from my publishing gig, with a hazy vision of becoming happily self-employed, I landed in spring with no clear idea of what I really wanted and no income. I reluctantly decided to hop on the treadmill again and began sending out resumes exactly one week before my son left the world.

But life is motion. Even if you are just sitting on the banks of a river lost in thought, your mind is in travel mode. This fundamental reality has not changed because I am consumed with grief, but my mind's ability to direct my thoughts into action through the familiar avenues available to me has precipitously disintegrated. What world is this where I can't work, read, create, laugh, or even open a fucking letter? Still, I must move. *I must find my son.* Sometimes, I need to go much farther than my legs can take me, and so I drive. With no known destination, for hours, roaming the winding, rural backstreets near my home, sobbing, thinking, forcing my injured brain to search beyond itself, searching for signs of Darby in the rising of summer, and, perhaps, my sanity.

I drive past our friends' large, clapboard house on a country road near a wildlife refuge—sometimes several times a day. Why? I don't know. It seems to be a kind of talisman providing me magical protection from the chaotic winds taking complete control of my life. Dan and I belong to a vibrant music community in our area, with a surprising diversity of creative outlets—art galleries, music venues, writers' groups—for such a relatively rural part of the state. This house is part of that community, and we have often played music together here—Dan, an accomplished guitarist, fiddler, and harp player, and me, learning guitar and mandolin to deepen my love of singing. Darby, too, was expanding his own musical circle in Amherst, experimenting and recording with friends, old and new. I've dropped out of it all. I tried to stay, but my mind, heart, and soul have gone away somewhere, struggling to stay tethered to Earth. Driving past now, I wonder if I will ever again be able to feel the joy and healing that music brings.

Like having to shift gears on a bicycle while pedaling, I drive to keep my mind from derailing. I drive until I am exhausted with the effort of pulling myself back from the edge. Today, a sweet summer day, I park on a roadside overlook on Prospect Hill near Fruitlands Museum. I feel an attachment to this place. Maybe it's the outdoor sculpture capturing my attention as I scan the sprawling grounds. Or the history of this site as the home of a utopian community founded by New England transcendentalists. Or bringing Darby here for a bluebird house-making workshop. Maybe it's just the expansive view from the road.

Soft, blue sky greets me through my open window, the warm, green embrace of nature in its most motherly, soothing aspect. Other cars, a motorcycle, bicyclists come by, stop for a look, a lunch break, a stretch before moving on. Scanning the spectacular panorama of mountains, orchards, sweet-scented flowering meadows, and hawks soaring high above, I search for signs of my son. Or for a bolt from the blue that will release me from searching. Anything that will help close the gap between understanding and this terrible longing in my heart. I leave the protection of the car and walk a little way into the field, feeling what I imagine a patient released from the hospital for the afternoon after a long illness might experience. Sun a bit too bright, green leaves whispering a bit too loudly, and the desire to feel my son here in the beautiful world too sodden with tears for me to lift off. I stare ahead with an unfocused eye as people come and go, then reach for the tape recorder and my neglected journal when I am back in the safety of my car.

Dan, in his ongoing attempts to bring me back to some kind of balance, connected with an old acquaintance, an intuitive skilled in crisis counseling. I'd never visited a psychic in my life, nor had any particular belief one way or the other about them, but the tide carries me to her, and I'm grateful. Petra has offered me a lifeline, holding me in a soft cocoon of safety and incubation as I come to grips with my confusion. I've recorded every session with her, the tapes my companions on these lonely road trips. I listen to every word working its way into the battlefield of my thoughts, doubt stripped down to a simple metric: Does the word find its way in or not? I press the ancient tape recorder's "On" tab and turn up the volume. I listen, press pause, listen, pause—transcribing in my journal the words that keep me sane today:

"What do I have to learn from this?"

"That this is the most challenging thing you will ever be asked to do on the human plane, that is, to trust that your love is safe and that you, in fact, are experiencing grace as you never have before. It is hard to believe on the human plane that this is for the best, but your commitment to this process brings you to a higher plane.

Those who know this pain know that it feels like it couldn't possibly go away, and then, miraculously, it changes shape, it gets a little smaller, it moves to a corner of your solar plexus and your heart, and it leaves room for all the love and the power that you need to have a life. It will move because the life flame is stronger than even grief . . . So you change, then it changes, that's how it works. Grief, like anything else, has to move. Darby is still moving."

The life flame is stronger than even grief. Is that what keeps me here on my knees, digging in this hard-baked dirt? *Are you comforting me with bullshit, Petra, or are you telling me the truth?* I am not comforted. The pain train hurtles through everything seen and unseen, a private tour through my own consciousness, suddenly ripped off of its same old used-to-be. None of this comforts me. The suffering mind is a lonely wanderer, but my soul is all about the journey. It knows how strong I am, that I can survive. In some miraculous way, I know this even here and now, parked on the hill with my tape recorder and journal and confusion and loneliness. I send a grateful thank you to my friend Petra.

The Howl

Dan has called my close friend Chris and asked her to fill our window boxes with whatever flowers are left at the nurseries as June comes on. He needs to see life returning. She has planted a lovely mix of petunias, salvias, and coleuses, and I watch them from the couch, bending slightly in the breeze as Darby's gone-ness weaves through every sound and scent and image. Gone. But still inside my beating heart, inside my body. I need to do something. Anything. I remember a friend visiting the house soon after Darby died as I lay curled up on the couch, Dan standing in the living room in conversation with her. I didn't have the energy to get up or talk—my pilot light was out. She looked at me and said that the key for her, at a time when an unhappy marriage and lack of direction had left her feeling depressed and lonely, was finding purpose in her life. Even though her words floated away from my thoughts, they found a foothold, waiting until I was ready.

I decide to take up an offer and work with my friend Jennifer, who has an organic gardening business and has given me an opportunity to rejoin the world. Pruning, planting, working the soil; *I can do this,* I think. Digging in the earth and feeling the solid substance of organic material sift through my fingers, helping tiny flowers grow, absorbing the healing sun through my skin. But no. The creep of panic begins, my heartbeat accelerates, and I think I might pass out from light-headedness. Even here, outside, with the clouds above and the earthworms below. I apologize and tell Jennifer I must leave, and she hugs me before I drive off, dirt beneath my fingernails and a howl rising up from my center. I feel utterly defeated and emotionally spent. Where do I go from here?

The howl is fearsome, and I know where it is taking me. Back inside my empty house, I fall to my knees, head bending to the floor, and a banshee scream explodes from my gut, crying out loud for someone to hear me, to *save* me. I am absolutely certain in that moment that I will not survive. I know this because, as I conjure images of my lost son and collapse into an unbearable longing for him, an irresistible force drags me to the edge of an abyss, a black hole that threatens to annihilate me as I face life without Darby. I have been walking this precipice since the eighth of May, but this afternoon, a hammer crashes down through my wild-crazy thoughts, and I realize that I cannot do this anymore. I promise myself, *will* myself, *force* my mind away from this place. I will not allow my grief to torture me like this. This is not about banishing memories. Holding on to them is the danger. Holding on like a jailor is to relinquish your mind to the monster you just created, a monster that feeds on a primal fear of extinction. In this moment, I choose life.

Maybe I am losing my mind; maybe I've already lost it. The chronic, low-grade depression I have lived with for a good chunk of my adult life is a disappearing act: the actor—the self that ostensibly creates and reacts to the events of her life—slows down, slows down, until the pilot light just seems to go out, and the dance of life goes on without her. But even then, she still inhabits her body. As a child, I learned to insulate myself from trauma—as many children do—by psychologically walling off the danger. I wasn't a tough, outgoing kid with a strong sense of self and ability to accept help. How much of this is intrinsic personality or a byproduct of the trauma itself, I don't know. I was sensitive, thoughtful, and introverted, so I constructed a wall of invisibility. Where other kids might act out their fear through bullying, overachievement, or being the class clown, I behaved more like the small animals I observed: When they perceived danger, they stopped, froze, and hid as fast as they could. I hid in my inner world when adults around me fought, when I was called on to speak at school, when I had to "show up" in any real way. The trauma itself was rooted in abandonment and silence. I was five years old, with an older brother and a younger one, when my father disappeared from my life. There was no explanation, no comforting hugs, and no one to turn to. At least, that's how I remember it.

Despite all this, I had friends, a social life, and purpose to my life, no matter how veiled. But it wasn't a fully engaged life, because my tendency toward hiding stopped me and affected my sense of self-worth. I weaved in and out of depression. But where I find myself in this new day is not depression. Rather, some kind of obliteration, not of the world, but in the way I have always experienced my "self" in the world. In Plains Indian cosmology, the thunderbird is a large predatory bird of awesome power who, in one of its aspects, can dive to earth, clamp an innocent child in its talons, and carry her away from every dimension she has ever known. It feels something like that.

A few weeks after Darby died, I looked at the stack of mail mounting on the kitchen table and thought, *Dan is carrying the financial load right now; I can at least open the mail and pay the bills. No, I cannot. I cannot muster the focus to read or write; I can barely feed myself. Luckily, we have enough food to last us a month, thanks to our kind friends and family.* The ordinary, everyday routines and rhythms of my former life are gone. In trying to come to grips with what my mind finds literally unacceptable, I am in a perpetual state of panic. But life goes on, I am here, now, and life is calling. I need shampoo and cat food. The very idea of walking into a store as if my life were "normal," as if my son were alive, horrifies me. But this has to change; I can't depend on Dan to live my life for me. I will attempt this. I drive two miles to the nearest supermarket, morning sun bright as ever, and walk through the entrance, grab a cart, and start my walk down an aisle. I scan the shelves, the people darting in and out of my line of vision, the fluorescent lights, the endless expanse of aisles, chatter, noise, objects, and my mind screams out, *Where are you, Darby?* And I am lost. All these things, these sensations, this energy, I experience as an assault on my body from every direction. Heart palpitations, churning gut, tears welling up—I abandon the cart where it stands and leave, fast.

Yet, despite my broken condition—and this new phenomenon of panic attacks—I recognize somewhere inside me that it will not always feel this way: I have a body and a mind and emotions, and they will come together again someday. My mind won't accept this, but there is another well of knowing deep within: the brokenness itself that allows me to access this.

Nature Heals

On the other hand, stepping into the rhythm of the natural world eases the gravity of grief, much like the effect of immersing myself in a hot bath. I walk, either alone or with friends whose first instincts for helping are almost always invitations to walk. Grief is ever-present, but panic can't find me here in my long rambles along the local rail trail, in-town forests, along the beach at Plum Island or Nantucket, on the Maine coast, or the mountain ridge at our favorite camping spot in the Green Mountains.

Family vacations when our son was growing up were mostly camping and outdoors adventures. From the time Darby was a baby until he joined us as a college student, every year we made sure to squeeze in a long weekend in the mountains at Coolidge State Park in southern Vermont. Recalling the natural beauty that had surrounded us, from our lean-to on the ridge in the Green Mountains, to camping by the red-clay shores of Malpeque Bay on Prince Edward Island, annual trips to Acadia National Park with family and friends, December walkabouts on Nantucket, and road trips out west—every place my son left his footprint in the spirit of the place—I thought, *Well, there's another place I will never go again.* And I feel a freight train coming for me now: our annual trip to Vermont for a long weekend of hiking, biking, and music. I feel the pull of memories dragging me to a fearful place. I can't go. I can't.

Dan and our musician friends who join us on these trips gently encourage me to come, and I tell them (silently) to go the hell, but in the end, I choose to bypass self-pity and follow the energy I feel tugging me north to the mountains. Our friend Bill, the park's ranger, who had also experienced a profound loss a few years earlier, calls to remind me that the woods are healing, and I know in my heart he is right. Yes, nature heals. The spirits of the trees, mountains, ocean, rivers, sky, and all the creatures that inhabit these places talk to me and wrap their arms around me in a kind of love that flows everywhere, if I can only allow it to run freely within myself. I lose a little piece of who I thought I was, and in the distillation of my "self" to the primal elements, I find some ease in this borderless land, a space to breathe.

Perhaps that is why Darby came to me that morning a few weeks after he died, flying high over the ocean in Acadia; a moment of grace, a vision-dream in which I surfaced into waking consciousness to see my beautiful, smiling boy gliding freely and effortlessly over the mountains and ocean we had enjoyed together for so many years.

—

CHAPTER FOUR

TO COPE OR TO HEAL—THAT IS THE QUESTION
JUNE-JULY 2008

The Teacher Appears

I arrive at Aileen's door at the end of June on the recommendation of our friend Karen, who has led Unitarian youth conferences with Dan and Aileen. Past the initial weeks of shock and confusion in my mind, I am finally able to eat, read, converse with people again. I have tentatively ventured beyond the loving embrace of those who have been holding me. An inner prompting, bypassing my once habitual, contrarian thinking patterns, urges me onward because it knows it is time to "make sense" of this wreckage—whatever this may mean. My heart races as I ring the bell, not knowing what to expect or even exactly what Aileen does. Hope for relief, even if it's fleeting, has brought me here, and that's enough.

Sitting on the massage table in her session room, oblivious to my surroundings but absorbing a quiet and calming energy through my still shaky body, we talk about the trauma that brings me here. Tears are already well on their way to overwhelming me. I allow my emotions free rein to help articulate this strange new world I find myself in, as I explain to her that whatever defined me as "me" has come apart in pieces in the explosion of Darby's passing and are off floating somewhere, each experiencing its own trauma: my physical body, emotions, mind, and spirit. I have nothing to grab on to, no unified structure of meaning to make sense of what I feel. My markers are gone; I don't know who I am, and it terrifies me. I am living somehow out of time, while everyone around me goes about their lives as before, as I once had not so long ago. She looks with perfect equanimity into my strained, watery eyes as my words trail off and suggests that what is actually happening here is that I am becoming awake and will be transformed by this loss. In the midst of such suffering, this thought feels like an ember kindling in the darkness of a distant mountain—true and impossible at the same time.

She leans forward in her chair and pauses for a few moments, her bright, brown eyes focusing intently on mine.

"Did Dan tell you what I do? Does he know what I do?"

I tell her I understood her to be a bodywork practitioner.

"You do Reiki or some kind of massage?" Although I'm familiar with alternative healing systems, my practical knowledge of energy work is somewhat limited. But her question and the subtle way it changes the energy in the room rivets my attention as she explains that her clients come to her for many different reasons. They might be emotional: depression, anxiety, grief, relationship issues, a desire to change patterns, posttraumatic stress. Or physical: cancer, AIDS, joint issues, digestive concerns, diabetes. Or spiritual: connecting through the higher vibrations to explore, find answers, ask for help, or even just to have fun. Without revealing too many details, she recounts the story of a client grieving the loss of a beloved pet, unable to move beyond the loss. Intuiting that shamanic techniques she learned from Native American elders with whom she had studied for her own healing and therapeutic practice would be the most effective tool to use, the two worked together with positive results tailored to the client's needs.

She pauses for a minute and adds that, depending upon her client's needs, beliefs, the appropriateness of the situation, and whatever "shows up" in the moment, she is able to read energy in a specific way that has been particularly effective for some clients experiencing grief.

She then shifts her gaze slightly to my left and tells me that Darby is standing right behind me, embracing me, and telling me he loves me.

My body, unsteady with sorrow, comes into absolute focus, as if all that sorrow has been rerouted like a river through a door Aileen's words have just opened in my heart. The mere *possibility* that he is here in some way, aware of me and comforting me, changes everything. My son is standing behind me, and she *sees* him. A tiny but unmistakable subterranean sensation of relief flows through me, but I am at a loss for words. The day, the room, my attention have been distilled into this moment alone as I sit on the massage table, listening, absorbing.

Her kindness and compassion channel through an upbeat, expansive demeanor, and I immediately sense that she is more interested in mining the wild possibilities in partnership with her clients than holding their hands through sorrow. I don't know how I feel about this; I long for that kind of comfort, but something is exploding in me, and I know, even in this strange moment, I have found my teacher. She tells me that she knew Darby slightly from Unitarian church youth conferences—known simply as Cons—that she'd led years before. She'd shared a fleeting moment of eye-to-eye connection and recognition with him at an overnight social justice Con in Boston designed to raise awareness of the experience of homelessness. I love this. That she has seen into Darby's precious soul makes this communication with him all the more real and vital. My tears, gathered like an army in my chest, stand down as she shares what she sees.

Aileen works on my body first, diagnosing, asking questions about my physical condition, blending her intuitive abilities with her knowledge of alternative medicine practices to move the energy, interpreting for me what she sees as Darby's presence. She's explaining that she had seen Darby from the beginning and had never read from his energy that his leaving was a "mistake"—she saw only joy, a strong desire to help his friends, and absolute knowing that there is deep meaning and a kind of perfection in all our lives. He came to her when she was trying to decide whether to attend his service. He encouraged her to keep her appointments in her Nantucket office, where she would be of greater service to a client in crisis, especially when she already *knew* that he was all right.

But the tears will no longer stand down, raging back in a flood of blind grief. *My boy is gone,* and this, today, is too insubstantial, too distant, *not what I want.* I sit upright, unable to control these volatile emotions that have overtaken me. I move to rub my left hand, feeling a slight pressure, as if an insect had brushed it, when Aileen, sitting across from me, looks down and tells me in a soft voice that Darby had just touched my hand. He is now sitting behind me, his hands around my shoulders. He asks me to have faith in him and believe in him. He is sorry for what I am going through, but had to leave his body because it couldn't contain him anymore. Aileen tells me that he has tremendous spiritual energy and she is visualizing his body as a "rag doll" with his hand massaging a place on his neck—a characterization that resonates with me, as I always had a vague sense of his unease in his body. And the darker reality of his drug use that had resulted in a sore on his neck that would not quite heal, less than a year before he left the Earth, and that I now suspect was methicillin-resistant staphylococcus aureus (MRSA), an infection caused by an antibiotic-resistant staph bacteria associated with injection drug use. The shock of this has yet to settle in my brain.

Our hour—or hours, I have lost my sense of time—has come to an end, and my whole body is buzzing. Floating above the sorrow and longing for Darby is something like gratitude, as I allow every word into my heart without judgment for this space of this time with Aileen. It is clear to me that my relationship with her and the work we are starting is a direction in which I need to go. The knowing I had that night on my porch steps when I vowed to get to the bottom of what happened and to find my son is blooming in this room somehow today.

Grief Group

A troubling question hovers over all my searching: Is it really possible to heal from such a deep wound? After enduring Darby's first birthday without him on July 5, just two months after his leaving us, it doesn't seem likely. But I am driven. And manic. It's mid-July, the sun beginning to sink toward the horizon in a grayish sky as I take the plunge and visit a local grief group. I tell Dan about this group I want to explore, and he wants to come with me, but a work commitment prevents him this time, so I'm on my own. Once there, I know instinctively that it's too soon to join this group. If my body trembled in the welcoming space of Aileen's office, what will I feel here? But I'm desperate for relief from a grief I simply cannot live with. Maybe I can heal in a community with others who are grieving—or not. It doesn't matter; I just need to keep moving.

The group's facilitator welcomes me with the sad compassion that coming here demands—*So sorry you have to be here.* After introductions to the small group on this midsummer evening, we sit at the table, and one by one, each parent proceeds to tell the story of their child's death—every detail, up to the moment they saw his or her body, lifeless, on a mortuary slab. *What horror is this?* It's too soon—I cannot even think the word *dead*, much less allow myself to go back to that moment. The conversation moves on. I hear laughter and *normalcy* emanating from these mothers and fathers, all of whom seem to be far past me in the grief walk. I might take this as a hopeful sign for my future—and, indeed it is—but in my body, it feels like being hit by a rogue wave. Their eyes turn to me, inviting me to comment. I feel like an open wound that has been salted for good measure; no words can make it out of the hole inside me. We move on.

The facilitator kindly explains to me the guiding principle that the group has accepted after disagreement with the previous co-leaders, which is that people like us, who have suffered this most profound of losses, cannot hope to ever heal, but only devise strategies to cope. Coping—containing the horror the best we can. For the rest of our lives. I am stunned into silence, my heart racing, my mind waging a war within. I want to scream into the night with rage, despair, confusion. But I can only sit here, trying to absorb this message while rejecting it with every cell in my body as the women and men around me assent with nods and understanding gazes in my direction.

The meeting seems to be coming to an end, and a man, who I guess to be in his seventies, speaks. His twenty-six-year-old daughter had been murdered in a New York City subway twenty-two years before. (It turns out that all our children were around the same age when they died.) Often, when he travels through this subway, he has the visceral sensation that she's right there behind him, and he finds himself instinctively searching for her. This causes him such anguish that it still brings tears to his eyes. Despite his warm nature and welcoming smile, he is angry and resentful as he speaks. He wraps his arms tightly around his chest, his voice rising as he notes that a friend of his had suddenly died recently, and why, oh why couldn't it have been him? Without thinking, I blurt out, "But you can't spend the rest of your life shaking your fists at the world!" He quickly responds, "Why the hell not?"

I have nothing. I drop my head on my arms that lay crossed on the table, and my fellow grievers show compassion for me with a gentle touch on my shoulder as they exit. I get into my car and roll the windows down to this sultry summer night with those words ringing in my ears and my commitment to healing riveted into place. This is beyond my understanding. This man's visceral response was painfully believable and even rational, given that the most precious thing in his life had been brutally ripped from him. I cry for him, for all of us—his experience of such intense grief and love is his alone and not for me to judge. But within my tears is an equally visceral certainty coming from a source more powerful than my mind's ability to disassemble. New signposts emerging. I will not become that man.

Aileen and Darby

Despite my revelation with the grief group in July, on a day-to-day operational basis, I do not feel that I can heal from my son's death. However, in complete contradiction of that feeling, I sense at the same time that I have set my feet on a journey to find my son and myself, a new world. These feelings exist side by side. I have found an inkling of purpose to my life, although I cannot yet define that purpose. This journey chose me, and I accepted.

It's August, and though barely a flicker, something fundamental has changed in the way I move through my days. Although my grief overwhelms me on a daily basis, I can now count the condition of my survival in terms of months instead of minutes, days, and weeks. Along with the healing circle of energy surrounding Dan and me from our family and friends, my sessions with Aileen are an absolute lifeline for me. A kind of alchemy between the three of us is happening here, this space where Aileen talks with my son. I am weaving back together the lost bits of myself, and at the center of everything is Darby, then and now.

Today, as my body slowly uncoils on the massage table, Aileen sees Darby sitting under the bodhi tree, laughing and playful, encouraging me to go to a sacred space like a Buddhist temple or Hindu satsang so that the music of the chant will help lighten my energy. He is experiencing many things, meeting others, happy. He asks me to forgive him for what he did, but tells me that would not have changed the outcome. He wraps a prayer shawl around my shoulders and tells me that I am still his mom. He is experimenting with his power. He wants his dad and me to know that he's more than okay. Aileen says that, from the beginning, Darby was comfortable with his transition: no shock, or sense of the accidental, that it was a mistake. What she tuned into coming from him and unleashed in this "place" was a great well of compassion and desire to help others.

I listen, absorb, question, protest, and constantly come up against my resistance to such a belief system. Why should I believe this? Why should I believe that these are Darby's words translated through her? But always, I fall out of that thought-tree with a powerful sense of inner knowing expressed not just in thought, but in images and feeling, things I had previously dismissed as "just" imaginary. But a habituated mind that has been rocked by trauma and split open—well, the water is free to roam where it will as it creates new pathways.

I asked Aileen after our first meeting just *what* she was seeing, *how* she was seeing it; whether she thought she was seeing his "essential self." She described the process through her own skeptical nature in an email:

> I have often asked myself, *Am I really seeing someone/the deceased person as separate, or am I just reading the energy of the client and what s/he wants or remembers?* From all my experiences, admitting that I know nothing for sure, I do believe that I am keying into Darby, wherever he may be . . . whatever his energy looks like. There are many stories of different incidents, some with no "confirmation" for a skeptic on this plane in this point in time . . . and others with confirmation that used to make me hide under my covers! I "read" energy, and I do believe I am "reading"

Darby. What it all means I cannot say . . . Darby is near enough and his energy is clear enough that I can see him and feel him and hear him . . . and I translate that the best I can. That is all I "think" I know!

Have I been so severely compromised with grief that my major goal is comfort at any cost? I might have thought so before grief brought me here. "*That poor, vulnerable mother preyed upon by cynical quacks.*" For myself, and probably all those who grieve deeply and dive into grief wholeheartedly, the cheap comfort of a soothing lie just doesn't cut it. This is by far the most difficult work I have ever done. Because so much deep and painstaking effort is involved in survival and healing, it often results in the mind being broken open to a degree that it has expanded beyond previously known borders. Yes, my mind was broken *open*, but never *broken*—it simply switched gears out of necessity to meet the challenges of a spiritual crisis beyond its habitual ken.

Shamanism

In what seems to be another lifetime, I had decided to apply to Harvard Divinity School (HDS). Dan and I had both returned to school to finish our BAs at UMass Boston when Darby was a toddler. For that first year, we all drove to school together, and although it was tough emotionally, strategically, and financially, the three of us spending so much time together, stuck in traffic every morning on the Southeast Expressway, walking a path along Boston Harbor at lunch, hanging out with the kiddies in Darby's preschool on campus, was kind of wonderful.

After graduating with a self-designed degree in religion and anthropology, I had no idea what I wanted to do, but I knew what interested me, and when my advisor suggested that I belonged at HDS, I went for it and got in. As much as I enjoyed studying all religious traditions, it was indigenous cosmologies and cultures, ancient and modern, that interested me most. Each semester, I checked Harvard's anthropology department catalog as well as HDS courses, hunting for courses that excited me. The study of shamanism and its worldview within an academic framework—from its origins in ancient Siberia to modern-day cultures from the Americas to Africa—points to a common thread within its diverse forms: a belief in the interconnection of all living things and access to an unseen world powering it, which shamans throughout recorded history have manipulated for healing and teaching. This is what drew me in. So, yes, it turns out I went to Harvard, of all places, to study shamanism. That was then.

On this August night, I feel a strong desire to attempt to go into the "dreaming," as shamanic journeying is sometimes called. For several years, I had been practicing journeying, an ancient healing method for accessing the wisdom and knowledge of the higher self and the realms of reality outside the doors of normal perception. But it has been impossible since Darby died. I am too consumed with his loss to be the open door necessary to welcome him in. I try anyway.

Immersed in fragrant bath water, I go through my rituals, set my intention, and descend deep into silence with rhythmic breathing. Darby pops into my mind. I banish him; I don't wish to be simply daydreaming here. He comes again, a smile on his face, and says, "I bet you thought you were just making this up!" I let him stay this time. We are sitting in a kind of twilight place, outside. He looks at me with compassion and says something to the effect that it had to be this way, and puts his arms around me. I feel the texture of his face, his hair, the pressure of his embrace, the deep look in his eyes, as he tells me that I will be okay. I am so happy to feel him, to see him, and so filled with sorrow. I don't know if this is real.

I keep an email Aileen sent me a few weeks after we met and

read it whenever I feel myself spiraling towards darkness, which was frequent in the beginning. It is another item in my collection of talismans: the great blue heron feather from Lee, the angel pendant my mother slipped into my hand the day after Darby died, a John O'Donohue quote. Searching for a way to go forward with my life at the time, I asked Aileen for her thoughts on why we come into these physical lives. This was her response:

> So far, what I seem to understand is that we are in these human bodies to experience all aspects of life as these human creatures . . . the feelings . . . all of them. For some reason those of us here lined up to get into the game . . . not unlike a sports game. In a sports game there are so many moments of hard work, emotions, highs and lows, angst, exhilaration and learning, adapting. When the game is over, we go "home." We were ready for this game this time around and knew all of the possibilities and aspects of playing in it. We all go home to the same house after we play our game . . . maybe some people want to play again because they want to get better at something . . . maybe they want to come back because they really love it . . . maybe they return to help coach or be captains of a team (like a bodhisattva) . . . this is just the game part . . . and it is serious when we are in it . . . because it means something to us . . . it is important . . . however, it isn't our total experience forever . . . we have a multitude of experiences if we choose to see them, engage with them . . . even play in them!
>
> Time takes on a new meaning, a new perception when we are in crisis and deep sorrow. This is a spiritual journey that transforms the way we exist in the world.
>
> Creating a new relationship to and understanding of time is part of this journey.

CHAPTER FIVE

Searching

Summer beauty is everywhere. Trees are in full flower, day lilies bloom in colored succession, rain refreshes the air and sweeps the sticky, yellow pollen away, birds sing like crazy. I look out the kitchen window to take it all in, but I'm sidetracked by the empty driveway. Darby's car, the old two-door Honda with bucket seats and state-of-the-art stereo system that would announce his arrival is no longer there. Another wave is coming for me, as I visualize him coming through the kitchen door, sleeves of his favorite red hoodie pushed up to the elbow, revealing a tree of life winding around his forearm—I don't like tattoos, but had to admit, that was a beauty. A quick hug, a body in motion, laughter, ordinary words on an ordinary day—I still cannot comprehend this. Despite the heavy digging in the mines of my own psyche, I cannot reconcile his deafening absence with these transcendent, lovely summer days. Not yet. I cannot stop seeing him in my mind's eye, coming home again and again, each image capturing my heart and knocking the wind out of me.

So, I search for answers, relief, mending; because at the bottom, I know in my bones that this life I am living now is not what I think it is. I leave the house to go walking with concerned friends on the local rail trail or along the beach, into the woods, out to lunch. An aborted attempt to work with my gardener friend Jennifer. Make pilgrimages to temples of healing, sometimes alone, sometimes with Dan.

There is sacred chanting; Reiki treatments; Hindu satsang; Buddhist meditation; a tearful spiritual healing session with Qi energy practitioner Master Oh; waiting in a hotel conference center all day for a hug from Amma the Hugging Saint; Ellie, the medical intuitive who I could tell was afraid of my grief. I am grateful to them all, no matter the efficacy of the healing. After all, how could I know what healing means? If there is love in the giving, I receive it with an open heart.

After venturing out on one of these odysseys, I return home to a space I have inhabited for over twenty years, a space that today, to my tired eyes, looks staged—flat, still, dry. And I think, *Now what?* The story has come undone, its edifice taken down. There is nowhere I want to be—not in this house, not in the world outside. I sit in my kitchen chair, my eyes turned inward, and I see Darby standing at the counter next to the stove, laughing with his girlfriend while cutting up vegetables to add to the scrambled eggs he's cooking for breakfast. He's right over there, so close and substantial I could touch him. And I can't stop the cycle of these images that do nothing but pile on to my suffering. This passes, but I intuitively brace for the next wave. It does no good to realize with my brain that I will not always feel this way. Here, now, in this moment, I am nowhere.

Things from our compassionate tribe have been piling up in the house since May 8. Dozens of sympathy cards, food, plants and flowers, phone calls and invitations from friends and my brothers, mother, sister-in-law, nieces and nephews. But time goes by so slowly, not marked by the turning clock or changing seasons or predictability of a working day. So how do I get home? There is no going back to the same old used-to-be. My "disorder" seems quite permanent, and the task as I see it requires exploration of this inner territory on its own terms. Darby is everywhere and nowhere; intensely here, radically gone. Time as I knew it has been displaced.

Time

Time, as Aileen mentioned at the beginning of my work with her, *has* taken on a new meaning, and in *this* moment, it scares the hell out of me. The question: *How will I live each day of my life without you?* That is the question, the basic contradiction of my search for Darby, the reason I come to her door every week. I am following my prime directive; *I will get to the bottom of this and find my son*; and pleading with her at the same time to tell me how I am to live without him. I am both captive to time and catapulted beyond it, a stranger in a strange land. Who the hell am I?

I hear the muffled barking of Aileen's dogs somewhere in her house. I finally caught sight of one of them last week at our Wednesday session—Haddie, a rambunctious, happy mutt rescued from an unhappy fate, ripping up the fenced-in backyard and jumping several feet off the ground at the sight of me. She makes me smile. And then it hits me again. Life goes on here in this suburban neighborhood: barking dogs, kids coming home from school, Aileen herself leading a full and active life. It's where I used to place myself, but now I am on some outside looking in. But I turn, taking the comforting path up to her front door for the tough healing that awaits within.

We sit facing each other, Aileen in high spirits, an inviting glint in her eyes as always, and I feeling small and weighed down with uncertainty and self-pity. I feel in this moment that I am justified in my self-pity. Aileen feels there is another way. "Okay, but what about this, Aileen?" August is ending and my birthday is upon me. One more shitty anniversary to be acknowledged, un-celebrated, and added to the heap of mirror-reflections I desperately want to run from. Darby's death day, Darby's birthday, Mother's Day. She listens to me with steady clear-eyed compassion as grief takes my hand and I begin my descent.

I let loose. "Look at what I've lost! I look for him everywhere, and all I see is his absence." I know I am debasing myself with this pity party and half-want to smack *myself* upside the head to get a grip, but can't seem to stop. "Where did it go?" I ask her. "How I am supposed to piece together a life without him—"She stops me right there, before I can utter another word, and challenges me to think about what I am implying with my complaint.

"Really? How exactly can you 'piece a life together'? It's impossible to know what's going to happen. Isn't the idea that we can piece our lives back together an illusion? And what exactly are these 'pieces'?"

She asks me to map out this scenario. As if projecting it onto the wall of her office, I see myself clearly: a solitary woman forever walking down a sad street, in a bubble of unchanging grief and the death of dreams. A diminished life. A life created out of "what's left." As I describe this depressing scene playing out in my head, clinging to a future that's like a life raft spiked with nails, I remember once again that I am no longer experiencing time purely in a linear way, and the old and new ways keep smashing up against each other. There are moving pieces in this new perception of being here and endless possibilities—one of which is actually *creating* that dismal scenario. I just can't seem to let go of the comfort zone, even if that comfort is as cold as an Arctic winter.

These are not alien concepts to me, but my grief and desire for healing is pushing me beyond my mind's habitual loops. It's like swimming in deep water on a crystal-clear day when suddenly it occurs to you to look back and see how far away from shore you've come. You've been grooving with the motion, the current, feeling like you belong here, but now the motion has stopped, and anxiety starts taking over. There are moments of clarity, hope, and movement juxtaposed with painful emotions. When a wave of grief releases its grip, the outward motion of that wave unfolds a little each time to reveal a little more light, a little more space to breathe, a little more insight into what's going on with me.

Making my way home from another session of heavy lifting and discovery, my thoughts drift back to that night on the steps at the beginning of this journey to find my son. Thankfully, no one close to me has yet offered the conventional wisdom that I will eventually "move on" with my life. My life is indeed in motion, but I have no intention of moving on if that means moving away from the presence of my son; indeed, that would be impossible. And that's the paradox: my love seems to encompass more than the ultimate fact of death.

Time in a Bottle

As late summer stares at me with its fading leaves rustling high in the trees, as I move further from the day of my son's death, the pain changes shape. The grief both lessens and deepens. It sinks down into my body, stretches out across everything as I begin the slow crawl of fully realizing that he isn't coming back. Accepting the reality of physical death takes time to unfold; it cannot be swallowed whole. So, I make the now familiar route to Aileen's office, heart wide open, throat tight with emotion.

Aileen connects with Darby's energy right away and sees him yanking forcefully at the cord connecting us, an energetic link she perceives as expansive and having beautiful energy. In an impassioned tone, she conveys his message to me—he wants me to live. She feels more profoundly today what she has felt before—that Darby's message is part of an agreement he and I made on a soul level, part of a personal evolution to help me wake up. My whole body—physical, mental, and emotional—tingles in response to his presence, like an electric pulse that seems to animate the whole room. I feel him, the love I have for him, and the love he returns in these moments, but the war within still lies in wait. It is not just a healthy skepticism that requires me to understand how this works, but a deep insecurity that I am unworthy of having a connection that is so profoundly rich and insightful. When Darby reveals himself, I feel the change of atmosphere in my body, and then my mind leaps, retreats, runs a lap around my brain, and tells me, "Yeah, maybe." But for this moment, my thoughts seem to arise from a bigger pool, a greater consciousness, allowing that liberating energy to flood through my body and expand my perceptions without ego-commentary.

Aileen would laugh out loud, with her very distinctive laughter, at the idea of presenting me with a spiritual fact sheet explaining the rules of the game for my enlightenment. Like all great teachers, she offers me the gift of self-discovery within a safe space, equipped with tools she has uncovered through her own journey and mentors. Even if she didn't talk to dead people, this collaboration—which I believe is the essence of any effective therapy—would be life-altering alone for the opportunity to delve deeper into the nature of reality, the mind, and freedom. So, like my entire grief journey from the beginning, I surrender in this office—again and again and again and again—to the exhausting work of awakening. If Darby appears in this process, I fill up with gratitude and sorrow in equal measure and set my doubts at the door, because this is what my heart needs in this moment.

When he shows up, I ask questions. I listen. My heart opens to let any part of him in, and even though I accept the truth of it, even if just for a few hours, it can make the loss I feel even deeper. "What do you want me to do, Darby?" He wants me to build a sweat lodge with Aileen's help. "What?" I'm familiar with Native American rituals, mostly from an academic standpoint, but know nothing about building a sweat lodge nor have I ever attended one. But I'm intrigued and in a relaxed enough state to leave it at that. More to be revealed.

The session winds down. Aileen holds my head for craniosacral work, identifying and releasing blockages and rebalancing energy centers in my body, all the while in open communication with Spirit. I relax into a meditative awareness to allow the healing to do its work and, afterward, I sit up on the table, feeling once more that my soul has savored a difficult but nourishing meal. I ask her, as I always do, if Darby has anything to leave me with before I venture out into the ongoing traveling circus of my life.

"Don't keep time in a bottle, Mom!"

Aileen and I simultaneously laugh out loud at this remark. I see his smile and humor all over this, but it seems poignant to me as well. As this image materializes, Aileen sees the bottle at a distance within a vast expanse of meadow, and this image triggers for me a Zen saying, with a twist, she has used a few times in our therapy sessions. Chop wood, carry water, and then the beautiful meadow. Life is flow, and change is always, and sometimes you just have to show up and plow the ground unknowing. I'm beginning to see that every wave of grief that comes for me eventually lands me in a "meadow" of spiritual expansion, and maybe there is no end to this motion. Of course, I am also fighting it every step of the way, but that is why Darby's message for me today is so meaningful—the only real future or past I have is one that I create in my mind now.

I have a memory. I see Darby as a three-year-old, running through a field of wildflowers at Tuolumne Meadows in Yosemite one summer long ago, his hair matching the color of wildflowers and his overalls stained with mustard from the lunch we had eaten. We set up our tent, and he follows his big sister as she snaps pictures of this beautiful landscape. Everything is new, everything an exciting adventure for a little boy who finds the magic in the smallest stone and the biggest, billowy, cloud-streaked sky. I can love him, and miss him, and both smile and cry at this scene, but I don't have to keep it in a bottle and put it on a shelf with all the other things we inevitably lose in our lives, because everything he was to me, all that we shared as mother and son, lives in me in this moment, in the timelessness of consciousness and heart. It's home, where Darby lives, where we all live.

Today, I welcome the red-tailed hawks, the great blue herons, the hummingbirds; ancient messengers to this realm from the one beyond. I can tell when they are expressions of Darby's spirit and when they are not. I don't know how or why, or even what it ultimately means, but I have learned to trust this love-bond with my son. I may not be reading goat entrails here for signs and wonders, but I might uncork that bottle and allow myself the wow! moment, the synchronicities, and the teachings from nature to remind myself to stay awake for the gifts the universe has to give all of us to help us on our way. I can allow myself to say yes to the inexplicable, the startling, the magical, the seemingly coincidental, and let myself follow them down, and be grateful for the dead ends as well as the revelations.

—

CHAPTER SIX

MUD TIME
OCTOBER–NOVEMBER 2008

Dolphin Dream

With the October moon rising, Aileen suggests that I am moving into the "mud" of experience, primed for allowing the space around me to expand so the light can enter. But what is moving now is subtle. In this late afternoon, following a hard session, floundering in a seemingly bottomless ocean of sorrow, Darby's disembodied reassurance that he loves me isn't helping at all.

After the session, I lay down on the cold earth in my backyard to decompress. The golds and reds of autumn trees and the clear blue sky gradually come into focus as my eyes attune to the natural world, and I let go of the sharp thoughts in my head. My heart quiets, and the tension in my body leaks out onto the ground around me, blurring the boundary between my body and the earth. *Well, this is nice—thank you, Mother Nature, for rescuing me from my rogue mind once again.* I glance over at our half-finished house addition, then up through the tree branches to the fading light, and over to the other side, to the small house waiting to be sold on the hill behind us. I don't want to get up, where my thoughts will surely trap me again, but my body signals that it's getting too cold for comfort. The tears are done for now. They have done their scouring work, leaving a cleaner wound. Darby and I are entering into a new relationship, one not dependent on physicality, one that says that silence is not necessarily evidence of emptiness. The loneliness of grief begins to respond to the light within—hidden, but always present.

A month ago, as late summer began its transit into fall, I was visited in a dream by a pod of dolphins. I rarely remember my dreams, and even during this traumatic time, that remains true. So when one comes and is extraordinarily vivid and self-contained, I pay attention and add it to the story that belongs to Darby and me. In this dream, my grandfather drives me to my childhood home and then leaves me in the familiar living room to discern why I have been brought here. As he waves good-bye and exits the house, I notice his glasses are broken and make a mental note to fix them for him. I turn to the back of the room, where a large mirror rests on a wall, and see his chair in the corner near the window to the backyard. Night has come. Looking out the window, I am stunned to see several dolphins in the sky above the house. Other people in the room, more felt than seen within the dream-state, have a more pedestrian attitude, agreeing that seeing dolphins flying through the air isn't that unusual. They are silvery, translucent, not easily seen at first, and seem to be swimming in the air. Mesmerized, I watch the night sky through the tree branches and am startled to see two or three of the dolphins suddenly descend into my backyard. Our eyes connect for a moment, and I see how agitated they are—they cannot stay long on the ground without damage and soon return to the sky.

My interpretation is that the dolphins landed at the place where I was tethered in confusion and pain to tell me they couldn't stay where they didn't belong—and neither could I. They came to help me find my way through psychological chaos, to show me the wings I would need to ascend. And it was my grandfather, the man who helped raise me in his house, who led me here. Separation and death are in this dream, and beauty and love. There are woundedness and the possibility of renewal. I have found that deep truth and healing are in the language of mythic symbolism. It is here that I enter the shaman's world where such images embody a reality beyond words, accessible through expanded, or altered, consciousness. The wound that is almost imperceptibly healing in me feels like an opening, a window to this world, containing words and symbols that I can use to take myself below the surface of my life.

Shamanic Fire Ritual

A friend invites me to join him in a shamanic fire ceremony at a nearby metaphysical healing center on Halloween, or Samhain, as it was known to the ancient Celts. The ceremony is for healing grief and loss. It is performed at a time that, according to ancient pastoral people, marks both beginnings and endings, a time when the veil between this world and the "otherworld" is believed to be at it thinnest, and the dead mingle with the living. We sit in chairs and on couches in the dimly lit room, gathered around a coffee table covered with the raw materials to make medicine bundles for the fire. The facilitator, David, is an outgoing, charismatic man with a thick head of longish hair, neatly trimmed beard, and a seemingly smitten group of acolytes surrounding him. At his direction, we build our bundles for the ceremony and bless them before proceeding outdoors with rattles and drums to find our place within a large circle.

As we file outdoors to the fire ring, I feel the ritualistic energy created within the group, mixing with an undercurrent of sexual tension around the leader, and enter the night outside subdued. What I am looking for always and everywhere is relief from the seemingly endless pain, and the only thing that moves it a little is connection— with people, nature, and even the stillness within me when I can manage it. Connection, love—their power gets under my skin, even if it can't displace the profound loneliness I feel every day. A much deeper, almost tactile experience of interconnectedness is creeping into my consciousness despite my best subconscious effort to sabotage it.

With rattles and drums, we find our places within the circle, the bonfire sparking wildly upward through the black night sky. As the interplay of flames against darkness moves with the dreams of each soul in the circle, a picture appears in my mind's eye of a bonfire we built in a nearby field shortly after Darby's service in May. We walked in quiet masses the quarter mile from our house to the field, others parking along the narrow, winding road, his friends and family gathering under a starless night sky to be with him. Awareness of what had happened to this young man we all loved so much still lay suspended in shock as I searched the faces, the flames, and my own burning heart for a sign. I sat on the cool ground and struck the drum, an authentic Native American frame drum gifted to Dan and me from our dear friends and bandmates on Darby's passing. The more I drummed, the stronger the desire to send it around this gathering of loved ones, and as it passed from hand to hand around the flames on this night like no other, it became sanctified.

I sit quietly among this group of strangers as the night grows colder, the Darby drum resting on one knee, tuning into the ritual energy holding us as David invokes the creative force of the universe, beating his drum and praying to the four directions. I lose track of his words as my heart responds in kind to the beating drums, the dancing fire, my thoughts weaving in and out with the trajectory of shadowy clouds traversing the moon. Tears well up and then recede. *Where are you, Darby? I* feel *your presence here, just as I feel it everywhere, every day, and I can't change that reality any more than I can disappear into thin air.* Sorrow and tears are necessary for healing—they change us.

Black Elk Peak

November ushers in early darkness and the call to hibernation for the winter ahead. On my way to Aileen's this morning, my thoughts travel back to May and a lifeline I created for myself—tied to my incessant pleading for Dan's reassurance—that if I could make it to six months, the "worst of the worst" would be over. Yes, but not quite what I envisioned. I can now walk into a store without having a panic attack, and I no longer feel so nakedly like a stranger in a strange land, but it's ebb and flow.

Calmed through a session of drumming and dancing in the warm ambience of Aileen's session room, I sit in the stillness of meditation, opening the door in my mind and heart to whatever is present with me this morning. What comes is an image of Black Elk Peak, sacred to the Oglala Sioux and the eponymous mountain in South Dakota where, in the mid-1800s, Black Elk had his vision regarding the fate of his people. I tell the story of a family trip out west to Aileen, who sits on the floor with me, our drums, homemade rattles, and cedar wood sticks laid out on the quilt beside us. She reminds me that the natural world is also, and maybe primarily, my teacher.

Twenty years ago, after being deeply impacted by a rereading of *Black Elk Speaks*, I felt compelled to climb this mountain, then known as Harney Peak, and did just that on a family cross-country trip to the West Coast. Just before forest fires swept through the western states that summer, on Darby's third birthday, Dan, Darby, my stepdaughter, Wreath, and I dropped our camping equipment at our site in Horsethief Lake Campground and drove to Black Elk Peak. Hoisting backpacks, water, and tightening the laces on our hiking boots, we were ready. At least I was. Wreath, a fashionista, trendsetter, and world traveler at sixteen, was, shall we say, dubious. Dan and I were enthusiastic, and

Darby was delighted—who wouldn't be, knowing that tired legs and whining would get you a ride up on Dad's shoulders?

We made our way up the steep incline, stopping frequently to take in the magnificent western forest panorama. I loved hiking and climbing, but living in the Northeast, the highest I had climbed were several partial hikes in the White Mountains and annual hikes to Mount Monadnock, a 3,000-foot ascent. I was looking at over 7,000 feet here, Black Elk's vision having enchanted me into forgetting about that little detail. So, except for Darby who was enjoying the view from his dad's shoulders, after much panting, crashed hopes that the summit was "just beyond" the next peak-we-mistook-for-the-summit, and mumbled desires to toss our backpacks off the cliff, the destination finally came into sight. A surge of energy propelled us forward, and nearing the top, amid the browns and grays of the mountainscape, we were surprised by a bolt of bright red in the distance and eager to discover its secret. As we approached it, we were startled to see a stunted conifer completely covered in ladybugs! Dan set Darby down from his shoulders, and Wreath and I dropped our backpacks and sat beside it for a few minutes in awe of this dense, bright cluster of life covering the little shrub in this windy, sparse place. Expect the unexpected, and you will never stop learning in this life. Thank you once again, Mother Nature, for the gift of the ladybug tree.

The winds picked up, the gray-white clouds massed around us, as we encountered two women, the only other adventurers at the summit. We acknowledged each other with nods and smiles; words seemed unnecessary in that moment. I hadn't done much research about the mountain, so we were surprised to find a man-made structure there— an old stone fire tower, long out of use. Gliding off Dan's shoulders and full of pent-up energy, Darby darted through its walls, followed by Dan and Wreath, and I walked toward the rock face, searching the skies but barely seeing anything through the thick clouds and fading light. Standing there at the edge with my arms outstretched, I felt the swirling forces of wind, clouds, and mountain music, and found it easy to imagine the voices of the ancestors within this place.

Digging in the Mud

Aileen reassured me in the beginning of our work together that grief changes. And weekly communication with my son has been key to the changes I've been able to make over the last six months. Staying open to such communication, however, has been difficult. My skeptic's mind continues to stoke fear and self-doubt about the reality of his presence. But that, too, is shifting. Since the walls have been blown out of my imagined orderly universe, I find myself at this odd juncture between *then* and *now*, *before* and *after*. It is in this space that the force of emotional reality—the portal of connection with all life—carries me through and, for now, my ego relinquishes the steering wheel. I see this now. I didn't see it then. I am *feeling* my way to a new understanding of the limitations of ego-mind and the extraordinary implications of an unfolding universe. And now, the real work begins.

In Aileen's session room today, so familiar to me now—the violet-blue of the walls, the tall tree branches, stripped of leaves, bearing witness outside the windows, the comforting touch of a blanket wound around me—my heart opens as Aileen relays Darby's message to me: "Isn't my mom great?" He is present in my morning ritual of exploration and says that he wants me to survive and be fully integrated with life. He knows this is a dark and heavy time for me, that it is time to crawl in the mud.

A hiccup of laughter bubbles up as I think of my tall, spiky-haired high school–era son rolling his eyes at such a declaration. I remember straddling a bench on Pearl Street in Boulder on our last family vacation together in July 2007. Exasperated after listening to my endless waffling about what level of white water rafting adventure to sign up for, Darby grabbed the brochure, pointed to the class 5 trip on the Arkansas River and said, "We're doing this one!" I was not amused, but I went with the program and had one of the peak experiences of my life. Exhilarating, hilarious, and Darby had my back all the way; he laughed and said he would make sure I wouldn't end up pinned to a rock as the raft sailed over a seventy-five-foot drop in the river. It wasn't the first time our roles had reversed and he had played the watcher rather than the watched.

Darby seems very present today. I ask him through Aileen's mediation whether searching for all these people I have come into contact with who claim they could read him for me is counterproductive. The desire for contact and verification is strong when you lose someone you love deeply. But it's becoming clear to me that going to psychics is ultimately a kind of fruitless endeavor. What's the point? I don't want more reassurance; I want an ongoing relationship that I can access myself. He says they are points of a certain kind of contact, but that I need to keep moving, going on beyond these "points" because that is where he is. I love you, Darby. I miss you. Thank you for being here. All of the above.

Gratitude

On another forlorn, rain-swept November day, I enter the session room to drum music. Aileen leaves the room almost immediately, with instructions to simply feel my way through this morning, intuiting what to do and how to move, using the objects she has left on the floor as I see fit. The door quietly closes, and I begin to move, windows open to the rattling trees and blustery cold. Pellets of rain rush in with the wind, shocking my body awake as I whirl past each window, sorrow streaming through my body without having a chance to puddle within. Light the candle, repeat an invocation, and give myself over to the trance-like dancing alone, picking up drum, a rain stick, a tambourine as the music moves me. Lay on my back in stream of consciousness, which ends in pleading like a child with Darby to show himself to me. Then, comfort time alone, with blanket and pillow.

Aileen steps back into the room and, with minimal conversation, we sit down on the intricately woven tapestry she had spread on the floor and light another candle. She asks me to quickly, without reflection, articulate five things I want to see done in this world. "Change our relationship to honor the earth, end hunger worldwide, provide access to education for all. And then, gratitude." I focus intently on a square of the fabric we are sitting on; emotions, thoughts, and sensations aligned with the power of this unique moment. Aileen prompts me to declare forcefully what I am grateful for in the tapestry itself: "The muted color gray, its sparkling quality and diamond shapes, the ways in which it reflects me back to myself." I am reminded of what I already know: that the healing practice of gratitude can open the heart and ground us in the present moment where transformation is possible.

Exhausting work, this. I have the carrot—Darby himself—to motivate me ever onward, down that unlikely rabbit hole. If I follow this path with diligence and vulnerability, will its secrets be revealed to me? Contrary to popular belief, deep grief does not render people emotionally weak, "not in their right minds." Grieving parents and others, because of the intensely focused power of this wound, are uniquely qualified to see the world with eyes wide open, the illusion of material safety and righteous order forever stripped from them. The heart knows with sublime discernment what is real and what is not, and the heart—the consciousness that knows its connection to universal life force—rules when the wrecking ball comes our way.

With Aileen, I am fortunate to have found a guide who never promises me anything, never steers me toward a particular "philosophy," never holds my hand when a hard truth is needed, but whose transcendent ability to track the energy never fails to help me find a route to the next breakthrough in consciousness. I trust her. I want this for myself.

My focus comes back to the quiet room as the session winds down. Q & A time: I ask Aileen to question Darby about the possibility of past lives, a concept I have been open to, as with most spiritual concepts, but neutral about—I would cross that bridge when/if I needed to know. The idea is actually not very compelling to me right now—I'm not at all sure whether I would *want* to "come back," whatever that might mean. Darby, as translated through Aileen's reading of his energy signature, describes the possibility of a pattern of simultaneous lives lived in different time increments—all the same life, but in different dimensions. Déjà vu explained: Something is experienced in one dimension (for our human minds are limited in their capacity to understand multidimensional concepts), and something is experienced that has not yet happened, according to our understanding of time, in another.

On the ride home, I once again find myself feeling elevated and energized in mulling over these explorations of consciousness—always like nectar to a bee, but now, they serve to incrementally untie the knots in my gut. I am stretching away from "ground zero" on the waves of my awakening heart. Sometimes it takes me tumbling through rip currents, sometimes up here, above the fray. My thoughts jump to a book review I read this morning, which dovetails with the session I have just left. In *The Wheel of Time,* one of several books about Yaqui sorcerer don Juan, Carlos Castaneda writes that shamans saw time as a wheel with infinite grooves, our everyday life being one of them. Shamans could jump these grooves to other dimensions of time and space, their movement reverberating still. Well, it's an interesting thought to play with! The door opens to visualize human existence in a wholly new way.

The rain has turned to ice pellets pummeling my windshield and making for a treacherous drive home. Almost there, back to my empty house, except for my two cats, Lotus and Puck, who are most likely curled up in a warm nook. I will tell Dan about my communication with our son when he gets home. We run parallel grief journeys, but they are very different. Dan throws himself into work, both his day job and collaborating with others toward a solution to the opioid crisis. As a lifelong musician, he also continues to play and write songs, a profoundly healing balm for the soul. Losing two children has changed his world as much as it has changed mine, but he forges ahead while I seem to need to take a break from the world—from music, jobs, the day-to-day flow of a life—incubating a new life through writing and working with my mentor. This is mostly rooted in who we are as individuals, but I also have a suspicion that mothers, because of the unique nature of the physical and emotional bond, experience this loss on a different level, a different frequency, whether or not that bond is biological.

The thoughts of this day, my session with Aileen and musings on the way home, are grist for the mill, but all I really want to know is that my boy is safe, at peace, and *being* in the reality behind the dream. That the human lifespan, the tears and laughter and disappointment and love that he is missing out on, is somehow redeemed in his play for the ultimate freedom. That he is the personality I knew as Darby before he ever became the boy we brought into the world. That if he was supposed to be here, he would be, simply because that's *what is*.

I move into this space of knowing and move out; move in, move out, and marvel at how my body absorbs the dissonance.

Darby Dream

The house is quiet. Dan is at music practice, and calls from my family and friends have settled into a more normal routine. I am taking baby steps to reclaim music and sing with my friends, but not tonight. I am alone. I light candles and incense and slip into the bath. We are closing in on Thanksgiving, and six months have passed since Darby's exit from life here on Earth, a marker of wellness I created and clung to in the beginning to stay afloat. And it's true. The shock waves have subsided, the confusion cleared at the center of my being where sorrow abides, but new life is being rekindled there as well. Nothing is static anymore.

Three weeks earlier, my sister-in-law Joan called to tell me a dream she had about Darby, one so lucid that she felt it was meant for me. As I rarely dream of him, I hold on to these visitations like a buoy. She travels with me on this unexpected journey, and I think he showed up in her dream because he knows I will trust her. As I soak in the fragrant bath water, Joan's dream wafts over me like a cool breeze.

He appears as he did in life: tall, handsome, but with a "glowing" presence. He tells her that he is always with Dan and me, but that he is "tired of traveling back and forth." She believes he meant not that he was sick of having to come to us, but that it was wearying to him. Joan said to him in the dream, "But they didn't know," to which he replied, "But I did." She tells him that we need more time, and he agrees. She sees the three of us in a perfect triangle formation, with me in the lead, Dan behind me, and Darby to the side, between us.

Joan understands this as a message from Darby that, every week or so in the dreamtime, I will organize journeys, or "exchanges," to spend time with him in the otherworld.

Interestingly, around the same time, both Aileen and my friend Petra independently receive images of this triangle shape containing the three of us, which reinforces my feeling that this dream indicates something stirring in the deep river that flows beneath the surface of our lives. In a session a few months before, Darby suggested that Aileen help me create a Native American sweat lodge. Aileen had been given permission to perform this ritual for family and friends by a tribal elder in the Pacific Northwest with whom she had studied. She said that my sister-in-law's dream of Darby's "traveling back and forth" fit into the building of the lodge. The ceremony seems like a good-bye to me now. Perhaps it's also a hello?

She says that eventually my relationship with Darby, once I truly accept that he is no longer on the planet, will be more expansive than it could ever have been had he continued here. Although I sense she is right, at this moment, I can't fathom how.

———

CHAPTER SEVEN

Thanksgiving in Maine

Dan and I make plans to run away from the holidays and the pain they hold for us. After meeting my brother, Dana, and his wife, Joan, at Plymouth Rock on this Thanksgiving morning to stand in the shivering mist with the Native American community on their National Day of Mourning—a new element of ceremony, safely distanced from the ragged hole of our old rituals—we leave for the Maine coast.

I sit on my cushion, looking out over the Atlantic Ocean on a gray day and sink into weary silence. I am grateful for our friends' kind offer of their condo. I imagine falling away into the wild, wide ocean, feeling nothing but the perpetual rhythm of the currents. My eyes meander up the coastline, and I remember. It's so close I can almost see it: Ferry Beach, a Unitarian conference center, where we took a shy, reluctant thirteen-year-old Darby to his first Different Drummers camp. He wanted to come home with me. We said no. After the first meeting with his fellow campers and youth leaders, he was in love—with the kindred spirits, the beach, the sense of freedom, the spirit of the place. Ferry Beach, the same beach where his lifelong friends from camp held a circle and bonfire for him in July, his first birthday not on the planet.

I search the condo for something to read and find *Loving What Is* by Byron Katie, a book recommended by a friend on her own spiritual quest. I immediately flip to the back of the book to search the index for the terms *death*, *child*, *grief*, because I want the author to tell me that my son is still with me, that he is safe, that death is not the end. *Death of a child* has become my talisman to unlock the secret of my survival—in book indexes, web searches, newspaper stories, quantum physics, songs, poems. I am pissed at the author because she won't do this one thing for me. I am not ready for her. I am not ready to *do the work* of loving what is, of asking the questions that might release me from suffering. Here, now, I crave the living warmth of my precious boy.

There's the big, inviting cushion I left on the living room floor of the condo. Dan's driven off to the store to get dinner. I will just sit in silence and observe the deserted beach below through the sliding glass doors. Quiet my mind, breathe like a yogi, gain enlightenment. Before my first yogic breath starts its journey up from my diaphragm, I am lost in memories. It occurs to me, just as the familiar tug of longing is about to rise again, that I have a belief that I must suffer—I *deserve* to suffer. That I am betraying Darby by *not* suffering. One step forward, three steps back—so much for enlightenment.

Preparing for the Sweat Lodge

Winter—the fourth season without my son. Where others dread the dying off and retreating within, I have always loved the coming of winter for its dramatic changes, the blast of cold, snowy wind on my face, the call to go deep within, the feeling of inner expansion that comes with being in nature transformed by the white, crackling silence. Darby and I shared a love of extreme weather: High winds? Nor'easter battering the coast? Dark clouds swirling above with thunderclaps? Let's go out! Before he learned that math was involved, Darby had a burning desire to be a meteorologist, a storm chaser. To this day, whenever I am out in extreme conditions, I see him beside me with a big smile on his face. And I remember his request that I build a sweat lodge for him and our family. It is time.

December 13, the day that Dan and I have chosen for the ceremony, is just two weeks away. It feels like a monumental task, and I drive past the barren trees and gloomy winter light, seeking Aileen's guidance and reassurance at our session today. I sit on the multicolored blanket she has set on the floor for me, surrounded by shells, a smudge bundle, and a Fisher-Price sleeping bag exactly like the one Darby used throughout his childhood. I begin with a deep meditation and then visualization that brings me to a campfire burning in the dark woods. I receive guidance about *reclaiming my power* and how Darby is with me on this journey, but hearing his name works magic on me—dark magic that instantly triggers the long ache that has taken over my being since his passing, especially on holidays such as Christmas coming up. Rewind the tape, press play: *Please don't go . . . I am so afraid of losing you . . . If I release my pain you will fly away,* as if he only existed tethered within a tight ball of grief. I am so sick of this! Will I ever feel "normal" again?

I open my eyes, gather paper and pens on the blanket before me, and focus my intention away from my mind games and toward the ceremony. The words form quickly and flow with a calm intensity. This Sweat *is* about reclaiming my power—allowing the primal fire-energy we are all born with to emerge and flow freely. I gave all that away as a child who needed to create a bubble of safety against an ostensibly hostile world by staying invisible and silent. But the Sweat is about standing directly in the flow of experience. It doesn't matter whether I think I'm ready; this is trust-in-action. This is about Darby and about me, Dan, Darby's cousins, uncles, aunt, and grandmothers who love and miss him. This is to honor his life, to acknowledge the living bond between him and us, to heal us from his physical loss and also from the things that separate us from one another. This is to acknowledge and give gratitude for the love that binds us all together and the Living Love that is the universe. This is to understand and perhaps experience that death is essentially an illusion—a transition, or reconfiguration of energy, rather than an end. This is to let go of fear. My reasons for doing the sweat lodge come down to three fundamental wishes: to honor Darby, to heal, and to share this experience with each other.

———

We awake to dark, thickening clouds and the eerie silence that often precedes a storm—something brewing today. It is Thursday, two days before the sweat lodge ceremony. As we lace boots, wrap ourselves in layers, and grab the equipment we need to harvest the saplings that will form the ribs of the sweat lodge, we choose two different areas of woods near our house, each meaningful to the life we shared with Darby.

In silence, allowing intuition and senses to guide us, we walk a short distance from our house to the narrow dirt road leading to our first destination. Stepping on rocks that will shimmer underneath a swift stream next spring, we note the trees on each side of the trail and stop as the pond to our right comes into view. The path beyond this point eventually winds its way up to a summer camp that twelve-year-old Darby attended, with much resistance, his first Massive Con, a large Unitarian youth conference and general free-for-all. As his shyness receded, he came to love these gatherings, but I don't want to stay in this mental space too long, knowing how it will end, and my awareness returns to the task at hand.

This path is an old friend, and I love stopping here for a moment of meditative observing and, since Darby died, to see whether a great blue heron will suddenly appear in the gray-blue gestalt of the pond and woods. Everything we do today we wish to do with intention and a sense of the sacred. With a small prayer, we ask the saplings' permission to cut them, and thank them afterward. Our emotions are deep, complex, and mixed with tears, but we both agree that we need to allow their honest flow, focusing our attention on the world around and within us. We are done with our work here and drop the bundle of saplings we've harvested near the dry streambed for pickup on the way home from another wooded area up the street.

I feel my heart getting heavy as I make my way to the next designated spot. This is the field where we lit the bonfire for Darby last May. Dan and I stand for a few minutes, searching the surrounding woods for the remaining saplings, remembering. The shock wave that carried me away that day carries me still, but it has normalized, like the routine ebb and flow of the ocean's current. After harvesting the last saplings, we straighten up, trees and saws in hand, and look around us in the twilight, chilled to the bone, and wonder for a few seconds about how odd the world looks; one-dimensional. Well, of course—no light emanating from streetlights or windows. This happened to be the start of the notorious 2008 December ice storm that blasted the region, and put many communities—thankfully, not ours—in the dark for days.

The Gathering

Two days later, we rise early and start preparing for the ceremony before the family arrives in the afternoon. Feeling nervous and doubtful about my ability to remember what I am supposed to do and say, I look out the kitchen window and see Aileen and her husband in the backyard, chatting with Dan. Aileen offers to support and guide me, and I gratefully accept her help. Yesterday, Dan and I built the lodge on a far corner of our backyard, with the opening facing west, instead of the traditional east. Intuitively, Aileen feels this is correct for us, and I do as well. In our session leading up to the ceremony, she explained the ceremonial protocols, sacred objects, and manner in which the lodge should be built, and I will follow them the best I can, but I am acutely aware that we are not building an "authentic" Native American *inipi*, and that is as it should be.

Dan and I are both drawn to this ancient ritual for several reasons: long-standing interest in Native culture and worldview, intersecting lives with a mentor who is steeped in this knowledge, and of course, our son's prodding in a previous session with Aileen. As a child of nature—feeling most alive and elevated when hiking in the mountains, walking along the ocean, walking a path through the woods (my true church)—I have long been drawn to religious, spiritual, and cultural traditions anchored in the natural world. Even so, the idea of cultural appropriation and dabbling in something I have no *practical* knowledge of feels uncomfortable. However, even the possibility that Darby wants me to do this trumps everything else: he knows I will follow him down the rabbit hole, no matter what—this is the carrot for me—and if this request originated in Spirit, I would surely accept. The ritual began to materialize in my mind even then, my energy sparking within. This Sweat is solely for our family's healing, and we approach it with an attitude of reverence and gratitude.

Buzzed with anticipation and feeling Darby near, the four of us split wood, carry the rocks to be offered to the fire pit, and welcome family members as they wander in. It is a cold, raw afternoon, and I feel my mind, body, and heart open as I observe the land, the sky, the faces of the people I love. I smell the breath of winter and feel the rush of emotions flowing through me—*Darby, Darby.* A memory flashes through the layers of busy preparation: My little boy in his rust-colored OshKosh overalls, plaid shirt, and floppy blond hair romps into view with an apple in one hand and the other reaching for everything and anything to touch, to explore. Dad kept his bees in white boxes in the far back of the yard, where we are creating the Lodge right now, but in Darby's two-year-old zeal to explore, they were not far enough away from him.

You are howling! You've gotten too close to the bees. You scream for us to come and make it better. We do, with a little love and baking soda. All these years later, you got too close again, but this time, there was no way for us to fix you.

Searching for stones we can place in the fire, I feel my vision shift in a peculiar way. I look back at Dan, who is splitting wood and carrying it to the fire pit, but oddly out of synch, seemingly alienated from the others, in my view. Spontaneously, I visualize him stumbling through the backyard in crazy, winding circles with the wood in his arms. And now, I am back in a previous session with Aileen in which Darby described us as players on a stage, choosing our roles for this lifetime. And many of us, soul mates, choose to incarnate together for this play. He said that this was essentially a two-act play, and although he had exited in this lifetime, I still had work to do here.

As for Dan, Darby told us that he was a "throwback." Aileen and I wondered what on Earth that could mean. He shows her an image: Darby and I are on stage, earnestly playing our parts, and Dan runs across the stage, playing a kind of whirling dervish trickster. We ask him why he showed up, and he replies that he wanted to be in the play, and we all agreed. I can't say that I know for sure what this all means, but from the time I set my intention for this ceremony, I chose to set judgment aside, use my new muscle of seeing, and allow into my conscious awareness whatever wants to come. And this flash on the day of the Sweat feels like falling momentarily into another dimension, and I *get it*, the family dynamic between Darby, Dan, and myself. Astonished, I look at Aileen, and she just laughs.

She and her husband leave for their home to walk the dogs, intending to come back with towels to sit on in the lodge and support the ceremony. But I get a call twenty minutes later that Spirit is emphatically letting her know that I will be okay with this, and that I need to facilitate the Sweat alone. Spirit was right.

Ceremony

The pale afternoon light is fading now, and I start the ceremony. Calling in the four directions with prayer and gratitude as we quietly gather around the lodge's periphery, I release the words to the sky above and feel what I can only describe as Presence. The wind and the clouds talk to us in their way, and we spin those words among us, conversing, laughing, joking, crying. As people choose stones to be blessed for the fire, I hold one in my hands and instantly feel a perceptual shift, one that resonates within my entire body. Its cool, ancient power moves within the resonating chamber of my body, and I am content to just let it be. I know that indigenous cultures worldwide perceive all things as imbued with consciousness, but I have never personally experienced the living essence of "inanimate objects" before, and it's like a code being broken, and finally understanding that behind the "metaphor" is a living reality. Aileen tells me later that before she left the ceremony, she had the sense that when each of us placed a rock in the fire pit, we were calling Darby in.

Protocols are not kept—I forget to have everyone call in the fire spirits; the too high ceiling of the lodge turns the Sweat into more of a mild perspiration; we don't leave the lodge after each round; we bring a flashlight in with us (the lodge ideally is in total darkness, replicating the womb of Mother Earth)—but the ceremony seems to have an internal flow of its own. As night descends, I take the great blue heron's feather, dropped on Lee's doorstep last May, one of a few animals that began to appear in my life as messengers from Darby, and smudge sage smoke around everyone, starting with our friend Ray, the fire tender who will not be entering the lodge. The anticipation is palpable, and the mood is not somber but almost uplifting and energetic as we laughingly try to remember to keep a clockwise rotation while going into the lodge. When everyone is seated inside, I enter and take my place near the door flap with water bucket and ladle and the Darby drum resting on my lap. Dark space and quiet weave around and between us, and I pour water into the pit where the rocks for the first round are piled. Dan and I welcome each participant as I name them: Darby's cousins Heather, Johanna, Eric, and Mark; Uncles Dana, Kit, and Jeff; and Aunt Joan. We include the symbolic participation of those who can't be here, including my niece Emily, brother Robin and his wife, Sandy, as well as for Darby, and my stepdaughter, Wreath.

I plan, according to Aileen's instructions, to pour four rounds of prayer, each accompanied by a batch of stones heated to a radiant orange, which we will welcome into the lodge one at a time. The rounds, based on the shapes of traditional Native ceremony, include: a blessing round, a gratitude round, a fear round, and a healing round. These are opportunities for our family to honor Darby's life, to acknowledge the living bond between him and us, and to allow us the possibility of healing from his physical loss as well as from the things that separate us from one another.

Except, it does not go like that. The drum passes from hand to hand, steam rises from the center pit, and the ceremony's structure gives way to a free flowing sharing of our grief, love, observations, and feelings for Darby and the ways his leaving has affected each one of us.

All our family members, including our nephew Mark, who comes back into the lodge after helping Ray keep the sacred fire alive, speak from the heart about this unbelievable storm blowing through our lives. In one round, when the drum comes back to me, I start a rhythmic drumming. I feel the barriers dissolve and begin speaking from my soul, not holding back my tears, but in this heightened state, I also understand that past and future are conflated into the Now, and that means my son is here with us, always. As I sit in that raw, wounded, loving darkness, I feel him viscerally. Like a fingerprint left behind on a frosted window, I see him beside me.

And then the outlaw flashlight switches on. All by itself. As one, we stop in our tracks, pause, and laugh out loud. Johanna says, "It's Darby!" And throughout the evening, the lantern keeps going on and off, particularly when someone is talking about light and darkness. From confusion and sorrow to laughter and release. The ego is suffering, but underneath is the journey. Like a deer moving silently in the shadow of night, guiding us into this unknown world, our hearts and minds are scoured clean. Not for all time or in any final way, but for this moment, which means everything.

It's over. We all go inside the house to share a light potluck meal around the warm woodstove with my mother who, at age ninety, is not quite up for squatting on the cold ground in the dark. The group mood shifts, expands, and lightens, letting in shared "peak" experiences, even laughter, as we celebrate Darby's life in our own unique ways. The day winds to a close, and Mark pulls out a poem he has been thinking about, a reflection we first thought had been written by Nelson Mandela but later find out had been recited in his speech, but written by Marianne Williamson, "Our Deepest Fear" from *A Return to Love: Reflections on the Principles of "A Course in Miracles."* Her thesis, that rather than fearing we are not up to the task of shining our light in the world, we actually deeply fear that we are "powerful beyond measure" and that the world needs us, resonates with us as night comes on.

The next day, Aileen sees Darby everywhere.

—

CHAPTER EIGHT

THE CAVE
JANUARY–MARCH 2009

"Under the canopy we erect to keep our children safe, our own illusions bloom. The world is a safe and orderly place, *our assurances run,* and our own family is especially safe.

We, your parents, have the power to keep you safe.

Spoken or simply felt, this is the litany and the illusion all parents share. . . . When you cannot protect your child, you lose the canopy of illusions that have sustained you."

—*The Worst Loss*, Barbara Rosof

Darby's Door

The dead of winter settles in with the new year, and I write furiously in my journal that I titled *Field Notes*. I feel like an archaeologist of the spiritual realms and the buried cities of my own past. Writing is an essential practice through which I've been able to create meaning of the last year. It has saved my sanity, if not my life. The perfect storm of my son's death and losing my job has created an almost unknown situation for me as I find myself home while the rest of the world works. The calls from my family and friends have continued to slack off as the "crisis" phase has passed. However, the writing—and the confrontation with my shadow-self it has brought me to—has intensified as I continue to ride the wave that came for me the night Darby left the planet. It pulls me through the murky tangle of my days, not letting me wallow in stagnation for too long.

That first wave broke within the dark womb of the December sweat lodge when I woke up to what had been hidden. The astonishing realization that everything in the universe is animate—no beginning, no end—unfolded at the exact center of my crazy grief. Astonishing not because it was a wholly new concept, but because the destruction of my old life and habitual way of thinking freed me to experience it completely, unified in heart, mind, and body, at least long enough to understand its language in that moment.

But now, the sweat is over, and I seesaw between brokenness and connection. I stare at the new journal entry on my computer screen on this lonely, cold-bright day, digging for inspirational words to help close the gap between my son's absence in this world that continues to stun me, and the fresh, circulating air that is incubating this new understanding. I reach for another cup of strong coffee and pace the perimeter of my living room. Every now and then, when I lift my head out of the tunnel vision of grief-work, I am kind of shocked to find myself here. Here, at home, in the middle of the day, not working or interacting with people, without a plan for the future. I look around the room and note the blue, worn couch, the Darby drum resting on an edge of the stereo cabinet, the woodstove keeping me warm. My eyes rest on the door to Darby's room.

This door, like an experimental art project version of a yearbook, with every signature of every young soul who ever entered this room: *I was here.* Deep fissures and faded white paint mark this door, etched with years of adolescent potty humor, angst, and declarations of love— funny, raunchy, loving, X-rated, innocent, beautiful, poignant. This one wrote to you in angry lipstick and this one in bold, egocentric marker. This one scribbled a graphic poem that almost succeeded in shocking me, an unshockable veteran of the counterculture.

And here, written in the center of the graffiti, like a god's eye, your love for Sylvia Plath and Kurt Cobain. A watery image floods my vision; you, wailing on your blue Fender Telecaster, just like Kurt's, that your girlfriend bought you for your birthday, earphones plugged into your amp in deference to your poor mother's eardrums. Then, I loved your unexpected reverence for the dark poet and the sensitive, rebel musician, but now I think, *If only I had known the depths of your troubled soul.*

This door that swung open to so much young life growing up while also keeping so much hidden inside. Discovering only after the fact that my teenaged son escaped through the window late at night to join his friends in the woods, in the streets, at the magic spot where they all knew they could score weed, meth, alcohol, and the heroin that would enter his bloodstream years later and never let go.

The Cave

Ten months after Darby's death, a raw, gray day between the fragile ice of winter and the inevitable greening of spring, I lumber into Aileen's office with tears stuck in my throat. She greets me with high-octane enthusiasm as always. *Really?* I think. Something seems to be moving today, and I have learned enough in the past few months to allow it to just be.

Aileen leaves me alone in the room with a large poster board and a box overflowing with markers and crayons; the only instruction is to draw intuitively, without thoughts of color or composition. I don't really feel like doing this, or anything else except maybe falling asleep on the floor forever, but okay. *Sit still, slow my thoughts, allow them to pass.* I draw a deep breath, center, and follow my fingers to the first marker. Streams of color arise from, and all around, the eyes I draw, eyes shaped like birds or perhaps fish, and a red, heart-like flower just below. A creature emerges that is human, bird, spirit, with fire-flames caressing it from below, and all the energy is representative of the feelings I bring with me to the session—a strong desire to expel the pressure that has been building up inside of me.

I put the markers away. It's done. I close my eyes and see the spirit bird emerge and transform through color and fine lines of fire until it gently resolves into a blanket of comforting silence. Aileen returns. After a quick glance at my white bear fetish earrings, she smiles and says, "They have Darby written all over them!" This startles me, as I wear them specifically to feel close to him, and I remember the long-ago day when Darby miraculously found these earrings I had lost amid a throng of dancing, blissed-out fellow travelers at a Grateful Dead–inspired mountain festival in Upstate New York. A sweet memory and a hard smack against the reality of his absence. As my mind, shaken from its habitual loop of self-limiting beliefs, strains to reach beyond the frayed borderland of my consciousness, I obsessively seek reassurance that what I'm experiencing is "real" and that I could one day communicate with my son on my own.

"Yes, there is no doubt you will, but it will happen in its own good time, and that is different for everybody," she reassures me.

On the table for energy work, I stare at the ceiling, wiping tears away with my bare hands while I tell her of my grasping attempt to strike a balance between what I perceive as suffering in my body and knowing in my soul. I look up, shifting my focus away from the mental-emotional shroud I have wrapped myself in, and feel the strength of her gaze. It steadily holds me and my out-of-control emotions without giving an inch to my subconscious demand for her to *fix this*—to save me from myself. How many times has she heard this babbling cry for salvation, like a baby who hasn't learned yet that the answer lies within herself? I am safe here, where my grief can move where it will, and no one will judge me. These thoughts barely make it into consciousness, but they set the stage for what comes next.

"So, Aileen, I'm struggling to learn how to balance this suffering that won't let me out of its grip, with this expansive way of seeing the world that is being uncovered on a soul level, so that I can live my truth and purpose, that Darby's death is an integral, living part of!" I blurt this out in one long tumble of breath.

Leaning in patiently on her chair beside me, she nods in recognition of my fine soliloquy and then engages me in a rapid-fire, heart-centered dialogue.

"Describe how it feels, in your body."

"It feels like lying pinned in a cave."

"Describe the cave—can you move?"

"Of course not!"

"Why not?"

"Because it's a fucking cave!"

"Look around: Is there a bed in the cave? A door, table, paintings on the wall?"

"God, I'm suffocating here; please leave me alone . . . "

"See if you can expand the space around you."

She challenges me to explore the gestalt of the cave in an immediate, intuitive way, and I resist all the way. I want to scream at her to stop. Why is she asking this of me when it should be clear to anyone that a wound so grievous could only lead to a life sentence of suffering? Yeah, every trauma could be healed—but this one.

Nothing makes sense. I cannot bear this, my mind screams, I want this—*need this*—to be over. Where do I go from here? How do I *do this*? At this moment of peak despair, something curious happens. The movie stops. Someone or something has flipped a switch, and I'm no longer the star of the show, but sitting in the audience, watching. I see myself as Prometheus, chained to a rock, part of me eaten alive daily while my son flies through the clouds forever beyond my grasp. This is the essential script, cycling in a never-ending loop, killing me over and over again since day one. But the power of that perception has just lost its punch, and I feel my gut relaxing slightly as I shift a few degrees from uncontrollable suffering to *observing* like an anthropologist. I am still in tears, still embodying sorrow, but all of that has been overwritten by the Observer, who breathes space around the pain so I can see that's all it is—*pain*. Suffering? That's a different animal. The Observer, who seems to reside somewhere inside me and who I have been aware of at odd moments for most of my life, puts a hand on my heart and steadies my thinking mind so I can see this. I have no explanation, and I guess that's the point.

All my resistance to the possibility of healing—*even though I come here specifically to heal*—held in a tight ball in my center loosens enough to allow me to breathe in my newfound cave. For the past year, Aileen has challenged the web of suffering I have nested in, and her refusal to enable my wallowing within it begins to register on a deep, felt level. I begin to understand that my resistance is an unwillingness to accept that I have a choice of roads in front of me: living or dying. I could allow the new to flow in—pain and all —or desperately hold on to what has already transformed. Living deeply or dying by degrees? There is no quick fix, or *any* fix for that matter; this is simply an offer set out on the table by a benevolent universe.

Body Prejudice

I decide to stop fighting and drop my "But I can't!" script on the floor and simply surrender to this new wave of awareness and embrace this metaphorical, energetic cave. I close my eyes, fall into deep, rhythmic breathing, and relax into the silence of the room and my own body. Following Aileen's prompts, I use my imagination to expand the cave's boundaries and create the dynamics of motion: getting water and food from the outside, putting flowers in the vases, and adding a window to the door. I make the cave big enough and transform it into a safe place where Darby is always welcome, which Aileen assures me is already the case. In other words, I give my mind permission to row, row, row my boat, gently down the stream, and see what shows up. Such a relief!

While still on the massage table, talking with Aileen, an image forms in my mind's eye that almost makes me smile as I continue to feel the energy of disconnection from the suffering mind: Humpty Dumpty, smiling naïf, not knowing what's about to hit him, tumbling off the wall. But in my mental movie, he doesn't crack open, "never to be put back together again." He falls, over and over again, and I see that these are my thoughts, uncritically wed to the narrative of hopeless suffering. But they are not *part* of me! A slight, momentary shift in perception, but huge in its implications, and I grasp this, even as the tears begin to overtake me again.

Aileen has been kneading my collarbone, talking to it and administering pressure, as she senses restriction that needs to be released, at the same time that I have been hanging out with Humpty Dumpty. I am now acutely aware of the pain and think to tell her to stop, but instead decide to let this go as well, and with my surrender, it ceases to carry the label "Pain." This is just another sensation. Of course, it still hurts, but for this moment, I am not making up some story about it. I seem to be in a storybook frame of mind: catching a glimpse of the White Rabbit again as he hightails it through this new hall of mirrors—curiouser and curiouser.

So many layers of challenging perceptions: Can Darby really exist as pure consciousness, with his "Darby-ness" intact after the indisputable *fact* of his death, his loss of materiality? Does the cave image go beyond metaphor into a dimension of consciousness that acts as a crucible for growth? How can imaginatively expanding and altering this symbolic expression of my emotional state actually change anything in my grieving? What *is* imagination anyway? And how can I *not* be attached to my child? I chose healing from the very beginning of this journey and have also resisted it every day since. I am so tired. So tired of the battle within. These questions are like a falcon's wings, carrying me up and away from the fight, breathing fresh air into my lungs, and expanding the boundaries of my known world—new possibilities for healing.

I lift myself off the table and sit silently for a few minutes, my head buzzing and body energized from head to toe, feeling as light and buoyant as a kite over the treetops. I look at Aileen sitting on her chair, smiling like the Cheshire Cat.

"I think when I was telling you my idea of 'balancing' grief in one hand and awareness of the big picture in the other hand, that wasn't quite right. Right now, I'm flying! Is this what you mean by 'raising your vibration'?" We both laugh.

I go on. "It just occurs to me now that it's more about *integration* than balancing, you know? It's like, I'm holding my *sorrow*, as opposed to my *suffering*, at the same time that I'm holding my soul-knowing. It's not really bouncing back and forth between them, it's more about integrating them, and I know that because I can feel the difference! Yeah, okay, I'm babbling now, but does that make any sense?"

I look up and ask my son, through Aileen's mediation, for verification of his presence, as always, with a mix of gratitude and sadness. An animated Darby proceeds to bust me about feeling sad that he isn't "here," telling me that I am "body prejudiced"—only recognizing someone when they're in body. Aileen and I burst out laughing; his point being, of course, that he is always *here*; where else could he be? "Yes, Darb, I hear you today!"

I am exhilarated and understanding things in a new light. It seems that what we dismiss as "just your imagination" might instead be a gateway to our inner world. Imagining the symbolic cave—in which I had buried myself—expand to let the light in, yields depth to what I thought of as the real world. Through this exercise, I've achieved a degree of psychological integration that has left a sweet, buzzing sensation in my mind and body—as if someone turned on the tap, unleashing a stream of sparkling water into my neural pathways, clearing out the deadwood, and putting a smile on my face. Not for long, or forever, but I'll take it.

———

CHAPTER NINE

GREAT BLUE HERON
APRIL 2009

Facing Heroin

Soon, I will not be able to say, "He was alive on this day a year ago." *Anniversary* has always held happy connotations: birthdays, weddings, balloons, celebration. But what is this? I still can barely make myself say the word *death* in the same breath with Darby, let alone risk the danger of allowing that day to consume me all over again. I still cannot fully face up to the aspect of his heroin use—the guilt of my self-perceived neglectful parenting unforgivable. I harbor a sorrow that he is missing out on living his life. I am not in a happy place today.

Darby had overdosed before. Two months before he died, he had gone missing in terms of being in touch with us. Dan and I had not heard from him for several weeks that winter, and after repeated calls, decided to drive to the campus when we finally heard from him. I was more irritated than worried, but accepted his excuse of being overloaded with coursework. Dan was less forgiving and sensed a red flag going up, but I preferred to sublimate it into more comforting thoughts. The night of his fatal overdose, sitting frozen with fear in a small, deadly quiet room near the ER, we found out what the problem had been. The doctor confirmed our worst nightmare—that our son was no longer with us. But there had been more. After a slight pause, in her brutally matter-of-fact voice, she dropped this bomb in our laps:

"You knew that your son overdosed before?" I was struck mute with shock, but Dan, incredulous, spat out, "Why didn't you let us know?"

"Well . . . he was an adult." The hospital could not have called us, because HIPAA regulations protect an adult's fundamental right to privacy in regard to their medical records and history. He was twenty-two. Several of his friends had also known. He had dropped out of their lives, too, in the weeks before his death, but they were conflicted about contacting us. Darby was ashamed and didn't want to hurt us. Two months later, he was dead.

I spent my blame on everyone: the hospital because of its absolutist policy; the university for abdicating its responsibility to the students in their care; Dan, for being too hard on Darby when he was growing up; his friends for not letting us know; the universe, for taking my son; and, most of all, myself, for not giving him enough support, enough discipline, enough love to do the one thing I was entrusted with—keeping my baby safe. So I shut down, and Dan took up the torch for justice for our son.

The signs were everywhere, but I hadn't noticed them. Even before the weeks-long phone silence, we both had a feeling that something was not right. Home for Christmas, he was sick, pale, and emotionally off-key. Again, Dan's radar was sharper than mine, as I desperately wanted to believe Darby—that his sickly appearance was just the flu, that he was overusing my credit card for school expenses, that he was continuing to do well in school. I created a mental-emotional bubble to filter these signs for my own shelter from the storm. I had avoided emotional conflict since childhood, undergirded with a subconscious distrust of myself as a reliable actor in the world.

But still, there were plausible explanations for all the red flags. Perhaps most of all, was the role—and I will just speak for myself—my unconscious prejudices played in my ignorance. Who used heroin?

Not middle-class, white kids. Nobody I knew. Despite the fact of my own psychedelic drug use in college in the late '60s and early '70s. *Oh, but no one I knew well used smack.* Despite being intelligent, educated, and well-read. Despite being ultra-liberal politically—protesting in the streets against economic and racial inequality. Despite my fair-mindedness and compassion, despite the fact that my love for my son cracked me open to a love for all children, I still somehow "otherized" some of those children whom I saw as victims of social injustice, but not flesh and blood fellow travelers in this world. It shames me to admit this, but there it is. Heroin scared the shit out of me, and I just *assumed* it did the same for Darby.

Turning it over and over in my mind at today's session, I confess my doubts to Aileen that I will be able to attend the benefit concert that Dan and I, along with many of Darby's friends and the caring staff at the Health Services Substance Abuse Center at UMass Amherst, have worked on for the past several months. As it turns out, the only date available for the concert is the actual date of his death. I just cannot face any of this. Aileen suggests I go up to Amherst before the concert so that it won't be such a shock on that day. Hold both the loss of him on the material plane and the inner knowing that the image of him I see so often in my daily life is truly him. Talk to him as I walk the streets and the campus. Let the tears roll. Own it all.

It is mid-April, and I have worked hard to clear a space within my grief to believe it possible to live a full, engaged life with my son missing from my life here on Earth. I remember Miguel Ruiz's words in *The Voice of Knowledge*, that a loving attitude, letting go of unexamined illusions, and rewriting your life's narrative in order to live an authentic life can actually *create* that life. It has been almost a year, and I'm just beginning to sense that spirit isn't just an idea, a theoretical possibility, but a felt presence that is palpable. I'm just beginning to feel Darby beside me, and to understand that he doesn't exist in my grief, only in my awakening to a more sublime truth.

Preparing for the Concert

I drive to my weekly session, welcoming in the unusually warm air through my open window, and commend myself for feeling rather balanced today. By the time I get on the table for energy work, I am crying buckets. It's the week before my dry run to Amherst, and I visualize myself traveling there and visiting all the places Darby had known. With Aileen's guidance, I close my eyes and enter a meditative state. I sense Darby standing to the right of me, holding my hand. He says not to be afraid of going up, and I say that I am afraid of my emotions. He shows me an image of a rainfall in the center of Amherst—the sun is still out, and it's only raining in a small spot, but the point seems to be in the flow of the rain. The raindrops come down, sink into the earth, and rise again. This is inevitable; it's the cleansing motion that is the point. Later on, Aileen tells me that he is saying that emotions are what make us strong. For me, emotions and projection are what make this so difficult.

Conversation between Darby and me flows this day. Aileen indicates he is telling me that I can't go on avoiding people forever. He means in the sense of truly engaging with people. As an introvert with a history of depression, I can't really argue with this. He says that going to these places in Amherst would let me see that the lawn in front of his house where the paramedics found him is "just a lawn." The hospital where he was taken is a place where birth, death, and healing go on every day, where people show up to help us. Go to these places with gratitude. He says to walk around campus and be happy that he had that experience and I helped him get there, and he was proud of what he had achieved. Given that, I ask him again if he couldn't have stayed—to graduate, start his adult life in whatever direction he chose. He replies, "You know, Mom, that wasn't our plan." A cloud passes across my vision, and I tell Aileen that I still struggle with believing that, but she says, correctly, that I *do* accept it completely, it's just that I continue to fall off into the grief piece, where "the plan" isn't relevant, only his absence. He also said that he could help me more now than he ever could have on Earth. I ask how, and he says by believing in him. Well, maybe; I'm skeptical.

Aileen reminds me that he sees everything now, and he sees my potential and capabilities. He says again that he can help me now more than he ever could have from Earth, and that he believes in me. He's ready to see me get up and out the door and follow my passion. She interjects how remarkable and inspiring it is that I, who have been under depression's thumb for so much of my life, could take this utterly devastating event and turn it into an awakening. I tell her that losing a child guarantees that you will look for that child, however you choose to interpret that, because that is what a parent does. For some unfathomable reason, that is what a parent does, even as death slams the door shut on that child's future. But it is like no other path I have ever walked, one requiring me to learn a deep, symbolic language, new modes of vision to see things invisible to the conventional eye, and a willing release of resistance to things that once kept me moored to what I experienced as reality.

Since spring first popped beneath the receding snow and as I dive down into deep learning, a pervasive sadness settles over me. Hearing Darby "talk" to me, even through Aileen's interpreting voice, fills me with a kind of long-distance hope, but the gap remains. It's the anticipation of a graduation that will not happen, and the exuberant youth of his friends that is no longer his, and the simple being-ness of this season with its promise of new life and a gentler stance.

Pre-Concert Trial Run

The next day comes windy and cool, and I need to move, to process, to work through the jumble of emotions fired up by thoughts of Amherst. No one is here this morning. I walk up the footpath that winds around the rusty gate into the J. Harry Rich State Forest, a few miles from my house. The layers of pine needles and winter leaves beneath my feet release their bracing scent, and the sun warms the breeze that sweeps the slow-coming spring in through the forest landscape. My face full into the wind, I turn left, to get a better view of the river and to see whether a great blue heron might make an appearance. My thoughts are in overdrive, but as the woods work their everyday magic, these internal ramblings break apart, give up their majesty, and just walk with me. Sometimes, especially lately, thoughts seem to enter my consciousness from no attributable source, as if someone planted them there. I am beginning to notice these things.

As the river comes into sight from the trail, a new thought comes traveling in: to believe that life continues and never ends isn't a comfort to get you through the night, but a portal that transforms you and allows you into dimensions of reality that you had no previous access to. It engenders compassion, unleashing love within you and to the planet. It propels you into motion—love in action. And at the water's edge now, I see the heron on the opposite bank, in flight now that I have come and disturbed its sense of place. Hi, Darby.

After Darby's death, I was given a book and pack of divination cards written by Jamie Sams and David Carson called *Medicine Cards: The Discovery of Power Through the Ways of Animals.* I sometimes pick a card to help focus my thoughts and get underneath the rote habits of my thinking. I brought the pack with me today and find the one I'm looking for: the heron. Its medicine is for those who don't know where they belong in the world. Heron "gently drops a feather" to guide them to trust their intuition, emotions, and the path ahead. I think again of the heron feather dropped for me at Lee's house last year, and yesterday's session eliciting the fear of my emotional response to being in Amherst and Darby's assurance that it would actually make me strong. The poetry of the words, the thoughts, the heron's flight, trickles down into my solar plexus without judgment. The wind speaks to me, *Keep up the good work!*

Time to go home. I feel calm and refreshed from my ramble through the woods, my mind not jangling or pulled in different directions. I am slowly reclaiming my life. I decide to visit a friend who lives near the center of town. He is standing on the sidewalk talking to his neighbor, and I wave as I find a place to park nearby. We hug, and after he asks how I'm doing, the conversation carries us where it will, and I notice how the emotional winds have shifted for me. Normal, everyday experiences—the heat of the sun on my arms, a neighbor walking her dog, morning glories curling up and around someone's porch post—don't cut me anymore, as if I didn't belong in this world because my son is gone from it.

Later that night, I tell Dan more about my last session with Aileen. He always, of course, wants to hear about communication with our son, and we share our insights, emotions, hopes, and fears. We are weaving a new narrative every day as Darby calls us, and that road is fraught with uncertainty as we try to orient ourselves to this new way of being with our son. It's late; the stars and moon glimmer outside the window as we climb in bed after a long day. My mind drifts, and I see the image that Darby showed me in the session—the rain falling down on a sunny, normal day, absorbed within the ground and rising up as invisible energy: yes, this is about cleansing. A new day. The rain refreshes everything. I would rather stay in bed tomorrow, but I know I won't.

Heron Medicine

I start the day with tears and a prayer. I ask Darby to be with me and support me. I ask the universe to help me through the day—to embrace the experience, whatever it brings, to let the heron bring its magic to me. I thank Darby, and I thank the universe. It's a hot, sunny day as I say good-bye to Dan and set out in midmorning, reminding myself once more to stay open to whatever comes. What comes now as I turn onto Route 2, heading west, is a memory. The last time I drove this road through Amherst to Hadley was almost a year ago with Dan, who had convinced me to see a play written and performed by some of Darby's college friends; a play he swore would heal a piece of me. I could see that Dan's energy was strong and soaring after attending a previous performance, and he wanted this for me as well. But it was far too soon. I knew I was too fragile, open, and raw to know how to process being confronted with the giant poster of my son, to whom the play was dedicated, as soon as I walked through the theater door. Or how to handle seeing his friends. Or even sitting still for an hour without losing it. Dan focused on the players and loved it. I was a silent scream, threatening to blow. I made him take me home. The narrow swath of strip-mall highway out of Hadley, its farmland on its way to extinction even when I lived here decades ago, was like facing a postapocalyptic landscape I had once known so well. Only the landscape looked exactly the same, and that was the unbelievable thing—*how could Darby not be here?*

I take a deep breath and bring my full attention back to the present moment and see the exit for Amherst ahead. Sunlight plays on my fingers as I grip the steering wheel, and I say out loud, "Darby was alive this time last year, but not for much longer." I can almost hear him laugh at the moment I say that. I don't know where the thought comes from, whether it is just my daydreaming mind, or whether he *is* laughing at me, as if to say, "Get a grip, Mom, death is not what you think it is, or what we have been led to believe!"

The four seasons have wheeled another round. I love the *idea* that time is circular and that all life is energy in transformation—no beginning and no end to any of it, including us. There is no real desire in me to search for proof, because that search can only lead back to itself. Darby just talked to me from wherever he is now, busting my ass for buying into a system *I don't actually buy into anymore.* To all of that, yes, yes, yes—and *yes*, of course, I want him sitting right here beside me in the car, tapping his fingers to a song on the CD player, telling me about a great movie he has seen, talking politics with an ironic joke, long legs stretched out under the dashboard. Deep breath, bring awareness back to the sun on my arms, the brilliant blue sky, my heart center and loving my son.

I make the turn off Route 2 onto the Daniel Shays Highway, and as I pass the gas station on the corner, my thoughts race backward to a wintry day over a year before when Darby and I met here to exchange cars. The twenty-five-year-old antique Celica his grandmother had saved for him—a sketchy rust bucket I worried about him driving—was his temporary transportation until his car could be repaired, but I was happy for any chance to see him. He looked tired, and I held back questioning him too harshly about his uncharacteristic overuse of a credit card I had given him as a short-term fix for a financial issue. Another flag raised, another eye turned away. I am not present at this moment; I am not in the Now because I am filled with guilt. But feeling the flood of tears begin their migration upward through my body, I make an adjustment, because I am on a mission today.

Questions for Aileen, or more accurately, a pleading for affirmation, for soothing, arise quickly with the surging pain. Can I really find peace with this and live life in wholeness and with purpose—the potential life I always had within me? Just as I verbalize these questions, fumbling for a pen and paper to quickly note them, I look up through the windshield, through the new leaves brightening the trees that line each side of this winding, two-lane highway, and I see it. A great blue heron descends through the treetops, its magnificent wings flapping slowly through the air, propelling it from one side of the road to the other just above my car as I pass under. Darby's messenger—I simply accept the evidence of my heart now and let it be. He came to me a few days earlier in the woods at home, and he has come again at this very moment when I feel a deep, urgent need to know that I can heal from losing him. It seems that he is telling me from his freedom exactly what is going on here, if I choose to follow my inner knowing. The message of the heron: dive into the emotional body; don't be afraid to go there. I think of the "falling rain in Amherst" image Darby gave me last week—growing, strengthening, and cleansing my heart.

Then, a remarkable thing happens. I am in a very grateful state of mind, not stopping the motion with the familiar "Am I just making this up?" script. Just grateful, for the heron, for Darby, for Dan, my family and friends who surround me, for my mentor, for the love in my life, for my tears, for my life in all its aspects. My window down, the warmth of a breeze embraces my arm, then my hand on the wheel, and my shoulders. The sunlight moves into my body. The leaves on passing trees rustle with incredible clarity. I notice, as if coming awake after a restful sleep, that everything has changed. Everything, and I mean *everything*, is vibrating in a sparkling wave, but that doesn't quite describe the quality of light that greets me. I feel in this moment the most incredible love surrounding me—I am in another world! I feel love rising from the pavement of the road, dripping from the trees, and in myself. All this begins after I see the great blue heron and call out its name. *Let go of your thought process and simply feel, letting your thoughts come along as they will,* it seems to say. Allow gratitude to fill the spaces that are mostly filled with sorrow, guilt, and grief. It unfolded within the space of a few seconds or minutes and then was gone, but I believe these rare moments, much like my altered perception in the imaginary cave, are encounters to another dimension of reality, given to us through the mystery of grace.

Back in the observable world, but stretched enough to let some more light in, I receive a clear message that I will be okay; I will be whole again. I am now at the highest geographical point in the trip before taking the right turn into Pelham and then the center of Amherst. I have always thought this was a magical spot.

Full Circle: Graduation

The drive into town is slow and heavy with the weight of my expectations. It is noon, and people are swarming the streets in impossibly hopeful summer wear—that's New England; the first taste of not-winter brings out the tank tops and sandals. But where is my son? My son who should be here with his kind, who should be meeting us for lunch and a quick hike up Mount Tom. The last time we did that we had a heart-to-heart conversation about relationships—how timing is everything and the fairy tales about love we grow up with can be heartbreaking when they are shattered, but end up giving us a gift of strength and knowledge. This was a young man who was maturing, and I looked forward to our unfolding relationship.

I make the decision to go straight through the intersection in downtown Amherst and wind around to the back of the campus, past my old dorm in Southwest—might as well stir up all the ghosts—then on to the campus center, where I park and begin my campus walkabout. I leave the warm sun and nostalgia behind me as I walk down the ramp and enter the cool, dark entrance to the Campus Center.

Scattered among the couches lining both walls are tables set up for a variety of causes and information. I find the one I am looking for: the upcoming concert/art project benefit for the school's Drug and Alcohol Awareness Center. There is no one at the table, but I look over the posters, materials related to the event, and resources for substance abuse issues. It's quiet. A lazy, steady stream of people of all ages fill the space, but—quietly. I stroll the corridors, absorbing the sensory flow, and turning a corner, I almost literally run into Elise, a dear friend of Darby's and one of the prime movers of this upcoming event. This is so unexpected and a direct connection with the very thing I thought I needed to avoid: the life that Darby "doesn't have" anymore. But we hug, we talk, she shows me what she has prepared, and it lightens my heart.

I walk the familiar path around the complex of buildings, where I attended classes almost forty years ago, to the campus pond where my friends and I illegally dragged a concrete tub to raft in the dirty water during a protest/party/be-in where a notorious yippie rabble-rouser whipped up the crowd, and the smell of weed and evidence of stronger stuff was everywhere. There stands the ROTC building that my coconspirators and I had attempted to occupy during protests against the Vietnam War. Memories of caravans traveling to Washington, DC, for the Moratorium March against the war and other caravans to Grateful Dead concerts up and down the East Coast. The era of shaking the walls of the old guard, of Buckminster Fuller erecting geodesic domes next to the dorms to experiment with new models of learning. And drugs. Drugs to play with, drugs to expand consciousness with, drugs to share and to explore—an intoxicating call to a young woman who had no idea who she was.

Walking, walking, now getting close to Bowker Auditorium, where the concert is to be held. I tug on the big wooden door and slip inside, prepping myself for an emotional response of some kind. The place is empty. I step into an alcove, take in the warm, stale air, and look up at the stained glass windows. And then it hits me: *Where is Darby*? I just don't feel his ghost here. Nothing. After a brief look at the hall where the concert will be held, I head out and make my way back to the parking garage. Through the maze of thoughts vying for my attention, I catch a glimpse of a young man walking past me, wearing a T-shirt that says "I See Dead People." I let out a huge, full-bellied laugh and send a smile his way! I came with expectations. I leave with a peaceful heart.

He's not here. Throughout the whole day, the thing I feared most, coloring Darby back into the picture I see playing out before me while the reality of his absence stabs me in the heart, never materializes. In other words, despite the bittersweet remembering, which is just what we do as human beings, I have very little sense that he is *trapped* here inside a memory. There is some third alternative between ghost and flesh that I can't quite discern. Driving home, making the left turn onto the Daniel Shays Highway, I am listening to the Kennedys' "Stand" on the CD player and a memory drifts through the music.

A few years ago, the three of us had met up at the Iron Horse in Northampton to have dinner together and see the Kennedys, a favorite folk duo of Dan's and mine. Darby's taste in music was distinctly different from mine, but he loved the Kennedys' energy and particularly liked the song "Stand." He was happy and healthy that night, and it made me smile to get the first whiff of the new, adult relationship I believed was in front of us. My memories may be attached to these points of physical materialization, but his consciousness is free of all attachments, and if I feel even a smidgeon of that reality today, I rejoice. There is something okay about that.

The strains of music weave in and out of my drifting mind—*Come on and stand, plant your sword in the sand / In this age of unreason / There's a time and a season for love, stand / I know you can*—daydreaming, thinking, feeling, listening, and another sensory perception breaks through. Darby and I are *never* going to be apart, and that thought feels like a flower unfolding in me. I look past the car window to the darkening woods and sky, and I see what looks like a hawk, another of Darby's messengers, appearing, bringing me full circle in a day that began with sorrow for a life cut short and ended with a realization that he has already "graduated." I flash back to our ride home from the hospital in Northampton that night a year ago and realize this is not the same journey it was then.

———

CHAPTER TEN

BE THE ONE
MAY 2009

A Surprising Request

May 8 approaches with lilac-scented breezes and warming sunshine that brightens the New England world with a gentle and jubilant touch. It feels like perfection, but the ever-rolling waves of grief pound me into the sand on this day as I conjure memories of my son coming home.

It is two days before the concert, two days before I face up to the facts of my son's heroin addiction and my failure as his mother to see it. From the minute I walk into Aileen's office, I can sense that Darby is all over this. The concert, the effort to bring awareness to this country's rampant, unseen heroin epidemic—its easy accessibility, its foothold in suburbia and the attendant cultural stereotypes it stomps on, the ridiculous cheapness of the stuff—is Dan's mission, his work in this moment. Me? I'm having a difficult time processing the heroin story. It is too personal, too fraught with devastating guilt, too dark to imagine my barely grown son grappling with such a monster. But Darby shows up for me today, with instructions.

After her hello from the top of the stairs, I walk up to the office and see Aileen in motion, opening windows to the spring air, adjusting the soft, background music, and lighting incense. She is wearing a funky pair of white cotton pants with brilliant red chili peppers imprinted on the cloth, which immediately lightens my mood. She laughs and tells me the story of how she bought the pants long ago and how she can't bear to part with them. "They seem appropriate today for some reason!" she says. We take our customary seats. She's animated as usual and has a particularly sharp focus as she tells me Darby wants me to engage the healing and recovery aspects of this concert's mission. Get AA and NA (Narcotics Anonymous) books for the table at UMass. Call Elise to set up a local AA organization information table and possibly a few people to be there Friday night. She says he speaks compassionately for the thousands of people—all good, "normal" people—who have died of substance abuse since the '60s. We need to give these people recognition, healing, and our blessings at the concert and stop our inclination to judge them and shame them as somehow "not us."

I tell Aileen that the reason this concert includes an art project component is to give students and others a venue for speaking anonymously from the heart about their own experiences around shame, trauma, grief, recovery, loss, hope. Bring this into the light of day with honesty and forgiveness and compassion. These hopeful thoughts feel uplifting to me but can't quite erase the anxiety and fear I feel within.

There is something challenging about all this. I feel challenged by Darby and by Aileen herself to not allow my grief to crush me or prevent my full participation in my life. Aileen makes me crack a smile when she describes the image she sees as I relate these thoughts: a giant Monty Pythonesque thumb smashing me down whenever I dare think I could be free of debilitating grief. For such profound, difficult work, we certainly do laugh a lot! I remember once again that I have a choice, no matter how often I refuse to accept this. So strange that the fog of depression I have dragged around with me for much of my life has been *lifted*. Darby's leaving has snapped me out of it and allowed me to find the fire within to navigate through grief and to see more clearly than I ever have.

Whatever all this means, I am grateful to be even a peripheral player in a campus event that encourages open engagement and is grounded in compassion. And because this entire journey has reaped such beautiful rewards, I once again open my heart to wherever Spirit leads me. I will bring the AA books, make sure Elise has the recovery table, and be present with the aspects that scare me as best I can. We discuss the possibility of offering, before the concert begins, a blessing or prayer—perhaps a ritual or ceremony—for those who have died from addiction.

And the last piece, the strangest of all, takes both of us by surprise. I have every intention of fulfilling his wishes—I have had enough verification of his presence by this time to give my doubting a rest, at least now, as I face what feels to be a difficult day. AA manuals and materials for Elise: *check*. A recovery table: *check*. Oh, and one more thing: Darby tells us that he, too, had to go through a kind of energetic process of becoming sober, and on May 8, it will be a year of sobriety. He would like a one-year NA medallion. "First of all, you're dead! What do you mean you are a year sober?" I look over at Aileen, who looks as perplexed as I feel, and get no help from her.

"I'm just the messenger!" She laughs. The prospect of getting a medallion seems impossible. The concert is two days away and medallions are given only to people who have earned them. I regrettably have to let that one go—sorry, Darb. A final word from Aileen: "Darby wants to thank you and Dan for loving him and let you know that he is always with you."

The Concert

I wake up with heavy emotions swirling around loss, memories, and missing him this morning, one year to the day of his death. My decision to go with whatever this day will bring might just mean surrendering to grief and its diminishing returns. Love, longing, and contrast between Darby's absence and the vitality of youth all around me feels like a vise on my heart this morning.

Dan and I arrive in Amherst in late morning. Another abundant, sunny May day, a lazy feel about it, campus energy at a stroll rather than a gallop. Feeling untethered and lost, I look about the sprawling campus buildings and budding trees from our parking space near the concert venue. No one at the auditorium yet—maybe a walk will shake the fog off. Yes, moving my body is an improvement; let's see what unfolds. My nieces and nephews arrive just after us and decide to walk around campus before preparations for the concert get going. I make my way up to a stone chapel I don't remember from my days as a student here and see Heather and Johanna turning the corner just as I approach.

We travel together for a while, first to take a look inside the cool silence of the chapel and then to the campus pond, where we watch the ducks and geese and listen to a chorus of tree frogs. It feels like a different little world in the middle of this huge kid city. My mood begins to shift a little, and I involuntarily laugh, thinking of what happened when Dan and I arrived here this morning. I share the story with my nieces while we sit amid this miniature wildlife oasis.

"So, after we parked, we opened the trunk of the car to unload all the music equipment. All of a sudden, this huge tree frog just leaped out of the tangled heap of cables and cords and beat it on out of there! Dan and I just looked at each other as if we had been hit on the head, and laughed out loud. Oh, well. I guess it was a hitchhiker from home, so we said good-bye and bid it a good journey!"

The three of us laugh and wonder whether the frog had traveled to his brethren here at the campus pond. Frog medicine for the cleansing power of tears. Yes, things are moving inside, but the veil remains.

Jesse

People arrive and begin to fill the building—the bands; our dear friends and fellow band members, Bev, Andy, Ray, and Ross, who have been there for us from the beginning; Darby's friends and classmates; my nieces and nephews; Sally and Diane from UMass's Department of Health Services; Aileen—and my emotions are beginning to overwhelm me with something I can't quite name. Everyone congregates on the lower floor of Bowker, where the kitchen and dressing rooms are located. I see Jeremy, Ali, Elise, Jake—friends of Darby's from college and high school, from UU Cons at Ferry Beach and Star Island, and from his after-school Whole Foods job.

Scanning the room slowly, my gaze comes to a full stop at a corner of the hall where I see Dan talking to Jesse, Darby's friend and Whole Foods coworker, the young man who sold him the fatal dose of heroin. In the rolling tragedy of the past year, the story of Darby and Jesse forms the poignant core. The drugs funneled into the campus and surrounding farmlands from Springfield, a large city about a half an hour from UMass. Jesse and Darby loved each other as friends. They were adventurous, invincible, and caught in a deadly game of Russian roulette. Jesse went to Springfield to buy Darby's bag and then left him afterward, as if nothing would ever change. His actions facilitated my son's death, and he went to trial and served a jail sentence, which was just. But I knew in my heart that the roles could easily have been reversed, and it could have been Darby who made that fatal deal.

Neither Dan nor I ever considered Jesse to be anything other than another victim in this tragedy and had no desire for vengeance, just a strong desire for healing and transformation for everyone involved. This upset a lot of people, including a few members of both of our families, understandably angry at the devastation wrought by Jesse's role in our Darby's death. But I am not angry. Maybe that will come in the days ahead, and maybe it will remain buried deep until I am ready to deal with that emotion. Here and now, all I'm feeling is bone-deep sorrow, love and gratitude for everyone here and what is being created here, no matter what comes of it.

All I can say is that revenge does not feel sweet. Locking him up and throwing away the key feels empty and futile to me. My son lived in this world, walked on this Earth, made a difference in his brief time here. To look for justice in an eye for an eye bargain feels heartbreaking to me. I don't speak for anyone else, nor do I judge anyone else. My desire for forgiveness for the players in Darby's addiction and death is linked directly to the need to forgive myself. Forgiveness so that change is possible. Otherwise, the road ahead is just dark and defeated. I want Jesse's penance for his part in Darby's death to be about healing and change, especially for himself: How might his actions then help create a world in which Darby and so many others could have made a different choice? That is the outcome my child is worthy of.

Dan has taken an almost fatherly stance toward Jesse; it was a chance to turn tragedy into transformation. But here, in this moment, I can't face him. I turn away.

A Sign from Darby

I search for Aileen, for a lifeline to the new world beyond this sadness, but she is helping out with the food arrangements and connecting with the kids—many of whom she knows through her youth work—and simply helping with her open and energizing presence. I continue to feel a bit lost, unmoored, not knowing how to help or where to go or how to be. I turn toward the door leading to the bathroom, a place I can hide out for a few moments, when I see Elise walking over to

Dan and me. We all hug, and she tells us in a subdued, confidential tone that there is something she wants to show us in private, before presenting it during the concert. We follow her upstairs where Sally and Diane usher us into a small classroom that offers privacy. It's good to see them today; I want them to know how grateful I am for the time, energy, and work they have put in, not just for this project, but for the all the ways they support the UMass community in promoting health and well-being.

Elise explains that she had created, with Diane's guidance, a video project called "If Only I Had Known." We gather five metal chairs around a small table holding a DVD player, and Elise starts the video. Music crashes through the speakers like ocean waves, and there is my Darby, in a series of pictures taken by Elise, documenting their relationship and time together, along with a heartbreaking narration—"If only I had known, if only I had done something, if only I could have saved him." How he drifted away from his friends, his family, his life. The life arrested in these photos.

After Darby died, I removed all the pictures we had of him from the walls and tables and put them in a box. I don't remember consulting Dan about this, I just felt that it would destroy me to see his face every time I walked into a room. The truth is, it took a long time to accept his death, and I felt, on some pre-rational level, that I had to protect myself from annihilation if I were to face the truth. I can now connect that to childhood fears of dire consequences if I stepped out of line. But right here, seeing those photos of Darby—with his friends, playing his guitar, being goofy, sad, outrageous, playful, lonely—fills me with a sadness beyond words. In this room, we are caught up in a rare and authentic moment that binds us together in grief and desire for change that includes and transcends my son.

As we reenter the ordinariness of the room, we hug and thank Elise for her amazing courage and work and wipe the tears away as we prepare to leave for the show. Diane is standing by her chair and calls out to Dan and me. She looks at us for a long moment. "I want you to have these," she says with a quiet simplicity, placing a small gift in each of our hands. One was her own one-year sobriety medallion and the other one she had in her possession from another source. I stand there speechless and absolutely *stunned*. This is the *one* thing Darby wanted me to get for him and the one thing I *knew* I couldn't do. In fact, I hadn't even told Dan about this request because it seemed so fanciful and out of reach. My face must reflect the shock I feel, because the room has gone silent and expectant. Looking at Diane, I tell them with a touch of trepidation about how crazy this will sound to them, the story of Darby and the medallions; that he requested them from "beyond the veil." A collective tingle goes up our spines, lightening the mood measurably and sending us down to the auditorium with startled smiles on our faces. Darby, you are a true magician!

Be the One

The concert is about to begin, and Dan and I walk down to the kitchen area just before going onto the stage. Aileen is still there, and I walk a straight line over to her, and, judging by the look on her face, evidently with the same stunned expression I exhibited upstairs. Among the din of voices and instruments being readied for the show, I enter a little bubble of quiet with her and open my hand cupping the medallion. I hug her, and she takes my hands as I tell her the story. We stand there for a few minutes in amazement—Darby actually made it happen! We will forever be grateful for Diane's kindness and generosity.

In the auditorium, the concert unfolds in streams of friends, family, and UMass staff mingling on the floor. The performers, so generous with their time and commitment to this project, play short sets after Elise's powerful video, touching on all the ways each of us can "Be the One" to reach out, help, love, and support one another and give voice to the fear and shame that keep us silent. It's our turn now, and with our band, Snow Crow, we stand on stage, the lighting blinding us to the people in the seats, creating, for me, a sharp sense of nakedness and vulnerability. On the other hand, Dan, who conceived and orchestrated most of this day, speaks eloquently about our son and the invitation to come together as a community, loving and supporting our children and giving a face to addiction.

As the music winds down, I say good-bye and thank you to several kind souls who made it here today, and make my way out of the auditorium into the hallway. I especially want to spend some time here, where the walls are lined with artwork created by students, friends, families—anyone who wished to express what they were feeling or thinking or experiencing around this event. The piles of poster board, construction paper, lined notebook sheets, along with markers and other materials provided by the UMass Center for Drug and Alcohol Awareness, are filled with poetry, messages, and illustrations where the anonymous artists could write and paint from their heart. I see expressions of loneliness, guilt, addiction, compassion, and desire for a community to feel connected to and protective of one another. One of them, with cryptic poetry and disturbing images, scares me a little. Is this a cry in the perceived wilderness, or something darker? But mostly, they are honest and philosophical, a few of them witty and others heartbreaking. It's another tale of truth in a night filled with truth and vulnerability.

The final piece in this emotionally volatile, exhausting day is a short interview with a local TV station about the emerging epidemic of heroin deaths among young people and our efforts to address it. I look at the young reporter, with the video camera running, and words fail me. I am overwhelmed by emotion. My friend Chris's phone call this morning floats to the surface of my wandering mind. She didn't know what it meant, or why she felt compelled to tell me, but the day before, a red-tailed hawk had been hovering around her window all day. Darby is all around us.

Is this a turning point for me, a coming out into this new world, having found some new signposts, new language, new purpose? All I can feel is *maybe*, but I don't know how to flesh out this word, and don't know whether I should right now. It feels like stepping through a hazy fog into a field of wild horses. Grab their power when you need it—it is the medicine that facilitates the next leap into the unknown. To quote the concert benefit's mission statement:

> *"Reflect, think outside the box, show support, and make connections. Be Creative! Be Loving! Be Courageous! Be the One!"*

—

CHAPTER ELEVEN

LEARNING THE LANGUAGE OF SPIRIT
MAY-JUNE 2009

Aileen, Darby, and Me

Spring is full-on, the one-year mark passed, the concert energy dissipated, and a nagging doubt that I have "achieved what I should have," which I guess is some kind of transformative experience, *right on schedule.* After all, the planets are aligned—the synchronicities, the signs, the messages from nature—and those things *are* part of a new language and way of seeing that is revealing itself to me. What is very old form, however, is how, like a driver on autopilot who speeds right past a new exit, I miss the signpost in front of me, habituated to the comfort of the old groove. My solution to this perceived failure of achievement? *Just try harder!* Lucky for me, I have a wise and skilled practitioner who has navigated these waters herself and is hip to my shifty, little monkey mind.

For the past year, Aileen has invited me to use our sessions as laboratories of collaborative, experiential learning adventures that might last a standard hour in her office or many more than that on the road to somewhere. I arrive at her office every Wednesday without fail, driving the fifteen minutes from my house with a particular focus I want to explore: a troubling thought, a breakthrough, a transcendent experience, a bout of heavy grief. As our session begins, she shares with me what Spirit wants us to do on these days. Before I arrive, she reads the energy, with no preconceived idea what we're to do, her ego not driving a narrative. And what she sees as our adventure for the day is almost always connected to what has arisen in my mind on my way over. The structure and flow of these off-the-grid Wednesday sessions have let me park my grief and heavy resistance to the side, allowing my curious mind, through intuition, intent, and symbolic language, to follow the rabbit trail. Both of us are surprised and delighted with where it takes us each week.

On this bright morning, Spirit changes it up, moving us out of the office and into the vibrant winds of the everyday world around us. Darby wants us to drive to a mall in New Hampshire, not far from us. I groan. Aileen groans, too, and then laughs. I am a voyeur/ consumer of shiny objects like everyone else in this culture, but prefer to do it outside the swirl of crowd energy and parade of sensory stimuli that seem to suck the oxygen out of the requisite brain cells needed to walk upright in a mall. But half an hour later, here we are, ostensibly at my son's direction. Our first stop is Marshalls, a discount department store. Aileen senses the color and size of an object Darby is leading her to, as well as the approximate aisle. As usual, I wonder how she does this. Because I don't fully grasp or accept how energy works, the idea of remote viewing and related phenomena are more of a suspension of belief than I want to admit. What I do know by this time is that her ability to track energy has helped connect me to a source of knowing within me that I have suppressed and dismissed. I never really believed in what we offhandedly dismiss as coincidences and lucky guesses, but now, the lines of communication are clearing up, and the desire to pretend is vanishing.

Elephants

Entering the store with curiosity and good cheer (at least on Aileen's part), we are met by a young blond boy in a stroller, his arms wrapped up around his head with a kind of look of forbearance on his face as his mother pushes him onward. *Well, hello, little guy, you sure remind me of someone!* I turn to Aileen with a smile, and as often happens, she creates an opportunity to shake me out of my ordinary thought structures. Proceeding up the closest aisle, she starts pointing to the outrageous stilettos on the shoe racks. We laugh out loud, laying out the scenarios in which we could wear these to greatest advantage in the service of having fun, and bump into two women who identify themselves as the Fashion Police. They advise against the gold plastic, tiger-patterned, five-inch heels in my hands, which makes me think of the clogs and Birkenstocks I have been wearing since Nixon was president, so I toss them in my basket. As we search for some cheap, funky clothes to go with them, Aileen suggests I wear this stuff for the next gig with my band—"Gotta shake things up, baby."—and I see myself on stage, with our jeans and T-shirted band, in my skintight red pants, gold lamé halter top, and shoes I'm not sure I can stay upright in. Well, it feels good to laugh, to be out of the grief zone, to feel normal again, no matter how long it lasts.

We drift through the store, up and down rows of dresses, underwear, packaged junk food, kitchen gadgets big and small, puffy comforters, and garden oddities, open to whatever shows up. I simply follow her, trusting her instincts and drawn forward by any possible connection to my son. There it is. Aileen spots what she has been searching for. I meet up with her in the aisle and see that she holds a dark-brown, wooden carved mama and baby elephant in her hands. I feel a knot in my stomach, and my eyes water as I tell her the story of Darby's first birthday away from the planet, just two months after his death.

We had run away to Quebec City, a country, culture, and language that was just different enough, just alien enough to wrap us in a blanket to insulate us from the worst of the painful winds whipping around us. I chose to spend the majority of my time in our hotel room's whirlpool; nothing could comfort me on this day, so what the fuck. The seven-hour trip up there was hard. Too much time to think, to remember, and be bombarded with the reality of our beloved son, gone. Blur outside the car window, discord within my body. I made Dan stop the car at one point because I was spiraling to god knows where, and I jumped out and just stood by the side of the car, crying hysterically. He held me, both comforting me and exasperated with how out of control I was. He was grieving, too, but seemed to find meaning and direction in the doing of these things.

Late in the afternoon, Dan slipped out and returned with a gift for us both: a sweet little candleholder in the shape of an elephant—we both saw the spirit of the Hindu god Ganesh in his face—to burn a candle later that evening for our son. The connection stirred by seeing this wooden sculpture on the store shelf today brought tears, but also a subtle joy in feeling the vibrating bond of an ongoing relationship with my son. Laughing with Aileen and the random people we interacted with earlier opened up the way to this joy. More gratitude.

———

Sitting in the backyard with Dan one evening, sipping slowly on a beer after dinner, the first anniversary of Darby's death freshly behind us, an open wound still, I start to drift off. This year around the sun has brought me to a unique and unsettling crossroads. When I visualize it, I imagine myself on a high hill, like a traveler in ancient Greece coming upon a pile of stones, a boundary marker presided over by Hermes, the god of transitions and guide of souls to the underworld. I offer my stone to the mound and stand lonely in the wind, knowing

I can't go back but unable to clearly see the path forward. This whole journey feels mythic.

After the Be the One concert, after the anticipation had been realized and participants scattered to continue their lives, after the music stopped, I sat with the question: What now? But it isn't about a goal, an object, or a state of being that will one day arrive. It's about a new way to live, a moving on that doesn't leave anything behind but instead pulls me into the truth of my loss. To fall in love with the life I have. Aileen suggests that Darby and I can converse with each other, feel joy, because he is still here. She suggests I think about reintroducing into the house all the pictures of him that I couldn't bear to look at after he died, not to remind us of his death, but to affirm his transition. Communication—with Darby, with my higher self, with nature—is subtle and takes discernment and discipline.

A Day in the Life

It is hard to give up on an old story you've been clinging to since before you even knew it as a "story." It's especially hard when you feel you have lost something so deep, so essential to your identity that you question your ability to survive without it. A few weeks after our adventure with the carved elephants, Aileen and I pack up the car with lawn chairs, a soccer ball, lacrosse rackets, plastic flowers, and books. She adds a couple of blankets gifted to her from an elderly friend on the Rosebud Indian Reservation in South Dakota, where she had driven a van to deliver much-needed supplies on the same day in November 2004 when George W. Bush's reelection rendered me nearly incapable of getting out of bed to go to work. Well, there's a lesson in the power of positivity! My reaction to external events and blindness to my own power to channel disheartening feelings in life-affirming ways is so ludicrous within this scenario it makes me laugh out loud.

Before leaving for our adventure this morning, she envisions the possibility of playing lacrosse at the Minuteman statue in Lexington after stopping off at the park's headquarters. But that picture slips the frame and arranges itself in another way. My sessions with Aileen are always open-ended, with the understanding that Spirit is directing us and that Spirit has a sense of humor. And so, we step out of our way and let the universe reveal its intentions on its own terms.

Veering off the main drag, we navigate our way through leafy side streets on our way to Lexington. The reason for taking these alternate routes does not immediately surface, but something about them connects to a memory for Aileen. Years ago, her children had attended a Waldorf school in the area, and one day on the way home, they had stopped to help a deaf Russian woman, parked by the side of the road with her hazard lights on, find her way onto the highway. We laugh at this sweet image, and from this memory and our discussion en route, which includes Aileen's story about her drive to the Rosebud reservation five years earlier to deliver clothing and other donations on a frigid November day, a theme about helping and healing seems to be emerging.

Along the way, we make another stop at her other office for the purpose of walking a typical day in someone else's shoes, whatever insights that might bring. This action feeds into a lesson about tapping into the energy around my own perception of expansion and life purpose. We walk the dirt path from her office building to Whole Foods next door. When he worked at Whole Foods, Darby used to bring us gorgeous wheels of brie and other delectable munchies for Mother's Day and other occasions. Now, I allow myself to hear Darby tell me what foods to buy. I relay this to Aileen without the usual caveat, "Well, I don't really know if it's him, but . . . " I am always digging, uncovering layers of what has been hidden for so long. Spurred on by the promise of finding my son, I'm weighted with grief as I dig, but also amazed at what I am finding with each new discovery.

We sit down in the store's café near a children's nook, populated with a bookshelf and basket of toys but no kids, and I feel my existence hovering between the light and the murk; it's a delicate balance and I never know which way it's going to fall out. Aileen, radically present as always, starts a conversation essentially about living a life informed by passion, without the mind-walls that derail the exploration we came here to experience. She tells me of the flowers she recently brought to her mother and how the dead mothers of two friends showed up, not to make any definitive statement about the afterlife, but for the larger point that I can either use Darby as an excuse for not experiencing joy and fulfillment or perhaps find a way into this wider world that wasn't available to me before Darby left. I look up because I realize I have been enchanted by a painting on the wall that my mind has not quite registered. It's a mural of two cute, blue elephants, a mama and baby. Aileen and I have a good laugh—*thank you, Darby*.

Hawk's Eye: The Circle of Life

On the road again, our journey continues on to the historic Revolutionary War route through Bedford. Aileen turns into the large cemetery on the right, thinking she is here to show me the gravestone of a childhood friend who died when both were young and how her death profoundly impacted her. But we immediately hear the sound of bagpipes getting closer and realize that a rather large funeral is going on directly in the path of the gravestone. From the car window, I watch the funeral in progress as we idle for a minute, and my awareness shifts from the individuals on the ground to its bigger aspect as an *event*, larger than the individual participants. This shift also has an emotional component, which I can't quite name. Aileen muses about some of those here who will be stuck on this sorrow aspect of death forever and the different degrees to which the various mourners are affected by this death. I think, *How far I have traveled in the last year.* Yet I feel, further below the surface, *How far I still have to go.*

As we weave our way out of the funeral procession and back onto the road, the Lexington Battle Green, the site of the annual Patriot's Day Revolutionary War reenactment, comes into view, and we see that the vision for fun and games on the green will have to be adjusted. An apparent reenactment of some kind is just wrapping up, and several men in Minutemen uniforms and tricorne hats, carrying muskets in one hand and iPhones in the other, are strolling down the common while a group of small children dance around the monument with butterfly wings on their backs. I sense Darby's innocent, little-boy spirit darting among them, a quick uplift to my heart. Butterfly medicine: Butterflies help people understand that you leave your physical body, which is a cocoon, and then your spirit flies. They remind people that the spirit is free, and there is life after death.

We look at each other and grin. Okay! Let's see what reveals itself. Feeling the sun's warmth on our backs, we walk slowly and deliberately around the green, simply observing in as open and receptive a state of mind as possible. Rounding the upper part of the common, we turn to view the First Parish Unitarian Universalist Church on our left, just across the narrow side street. Its roots trace back to 1692, when the first meeting house was established here, centuries later to become a Unitarian church. I know this church, having dropped my teenaged son off for overnight Cons with his friends from near and far.

We come full circle, back to where the car is parked and where we can see the contour of the cemetery in the distance. I feel a swirl of emotions, each with its own quality, as I note each chapter of what appears to me as a set piece: the reenactment of the Battle of Lexington and Concord that Dan and I had come to when I was pregnant with Darby. The butterfly children, who conjured an image of him as a young, innocent boy. The church, where he spent some of the most important moments of his life, a space where kids who felt they didn't quite fit in anywhere else felt welcomed. And finally, back to the beginning of this trip to Lexington, the cemetery, where dead people supposedly "rest in peace." I describe all this to Aileen, and she coaches me, as always, to not think too much, meaning my immediate tendency to want to *figure things out* in order to control and assuage my fear and anxiety, which are not really tied to external events. Keep the channels within me open and safe from self-judgment.

Her words begin to float with a lightness of spirit and merge with a spontaneous shift in my consciousness. What is stirring in my body right now is beyond mere memories. I see the scenes of my life "outside the box," in miniature, from above, as if I'm assuming the hawk's eye viewpoint of a creator looking down upon her creation. Babies born, playing with joyful abandon, sneaking weed outside a Con, finding love and coupling, working, laughing, crying, changing, dying. I see the endless generations milling about the church from its colonial beginnings and long before. I see them blending with the people walking these streets here today. But in this moment, these scenes project as events we walk through in our lives, rich with love and memories and meaning, but *not the essence* of our existence. They are ever-changing, fleeting happenings in the context of the infinite beings we really are. They are the experiences that create and inform the stories of these lives, but they are not *who* we are. We simply cannot be contained within the limits of time. Like the moment on the road to Amherst last spring when everything around me vibrated with love, this moment passes as well, but it has certainly rattled my awareness.

After I recount this new perceptual shift to Aileen, we climb in the car, both looking in the back seat at the instruments of fun and games we could have had, and once again laugh out loud. I feel very energized and centered and tell her what this experience has meant to me as I come into my normal consciousness and begin to reflect on this feeling of expansion within.

This deeply embedded experience of Darby I've been having lately, thinking that he has something he very much wants to tell me? Well, he's told me by *showing* me in a symbolic language far richer than the words I wanted to ask him today. How we walk through the events of our lives, including our birth and death, and that there is no beginning and no end to any of it. I saw everything as a dance of energy—*cells in motion*—that goes on and on and on, in and out of physical existence. And we never, ever lose each other. That is impossible.

In that moment, I am seeing through my hawk's-eye/god's-eye view our human milestones and everything in-between, not as the essential points of our lives, but as points of light through which we can love each other. That's all; that's everything. This all happened within a few minutes, a kind of teaching moment. As Aileen said a year ago, "You will change your relationship with time."

CHAPTER TWELVE

LETTING GO
JULY–AUGUST 2009

Birthday Message from Darby

This is the day I have felt coming for me for weeks, like an unstoppable train. I wake up to Darby's birthday this morning and talk to him in a pleading voice that makes me cringe. *Happy birthday, Darby; Dad and I love you and miss you so much. I don't know what to do with myself today. I just miss you . . .* I sob until my chest hurts.

After a meltdown last night, one that I hid from Dan, I emailed Aileen, desperate for some kind of comfort. Sobbing subsided, I open my computer and see that she has replied, in the form of her conversation with Darby:

"So, Darby . . . what are you doing today?"

Nothing . . . just waiting for my mom to get out of bed . . . a figurative bed.

"Can't you cut her some slack?"

Nope, she's my mom, and therefore, she must do as I say!

"Well, she's trying hard to see you and hear you."

It's not what she thinks.

"I know, but it's still difficult."

Aileen, it's only hard because she thinks she knows what I'm supposed to look like and what I'm supposed to say. . . . But I don't belong to her beliefs. You can tell my mother that I love her . . . I love her, I love her . . . but that doesn't change things, because she has to know that I love her . . . that I didn't leave her. I have things to do. It wasn't easy to leave the "world" as we know it because I knew it would make people sad, but there is a bigger plan. There is more that can be done when we go to the "other side" . . . So, Mom, I love you. I hope you get up and out and enjoy the day, because I am right here. Just talk to me, and someday you'll hear me . . . but talk about things you like to do. Hang out with Dad and spend some time thinking of me but not the whole day. That just weirds me out! How about a little bit of Harry Potter?

"He's laughing a lot right now. . . . He thinks he's pretty funny!"

Thank you, Aileen. I show Dan the email. He's much more willing to do something today than I am. So rather than stew in our own juices, we drive to the Nashua River and kayak for the afternoon, remembering times we spent on this river with Darby. Bittersweet is all I can muster. Later in the day, I receive an email from my friend Petra:

Today was such a beautiful day that I took a walk on the trail after yoga. I decided to come into Groton early on July 5 and do a walking meditation for you, Dan, and Darby on the rail trail. It was beautiful out, quiet on the trail, and on the return, I stopped at the bench by the stream and meditated there. That's when I could see you, Dan, and Darby standing together, forming a triangle. It seemed like you were all telepathically communicating, and there was a feeling of peace and communion among you. Then, Wreath appeared briefly and put her hand on Darby's shoulder, standing behind him. I hope that day was a good one for you. Darby was with you that day, and my sense is that he is centered now. Love and blessings.

Thank you, Petra. Gratitude is the light and the way.

We light our candle that sits atop the elephant holder we bought in Quebec last year on this day for you, close our eyes for a few moments, and talk to you, each in our turn. As if you were here. Tell you how the day went, how we felt on this special day without you, hoping you can hear us, hoping we can reach you. A little refuge, or calm at least, in the center of the crater you left behind.

A Serendipitous Meeting

Stretching Darby's advice to get out and enjoy the day a little more, I venture out the day after his birthday to find my favorite Indiana Jones–style hat I'd bought on our last vacation together in the Rocky Mountains. Absentmindedly, before leaving home a week ago, I had driven away with the hat still sitting on the roof of the car, where I placed it "just for a second." Feeling sad and angry with myself for being so careless with the hat, with its attachment to our last, wonderful vacation together, I leave the house with purpose, prepared to walk up and down my street to find it.

I have become a stalker of hidden things—the web of connections and its meaning, which only becomes clear in hindsight, if at all. What will capture my attention today, when the grab bag of thoughts loosens its hold? An intuitive tug, a feeling of connection to someone? Maybe a tiny metaphorical hello, maybe a loud *Hey! Over here!* And then, an *Aha, I get it!* when mind and heart are united in seeing the same thing. My little jaunt up the street, ostensibly to find my hat, is that and so much more.

It's a slow walk. Peering into the tangle of woods and neighbors' bushes, alternating between hope for finding the hat and anger at myself for being such a space-cadet. Hearing a gaggle of voices on this otherwise just-me-and-the-birds kind of morning, I turn my head and notice a yard sale in progress at the small house just up the street. I am tempted to walk on by and keep searching for my hat, but the tingling in my body catches my attention, braking me where I am, a few steps beyond the yard.

A few weeks earlier in a session with Aileen, she had said that Darby was showing her a brown house on our road, with woods and an open space beside it that Dan and I should visit. There may be someone in need of healing. I had immediately thought of Noelle, a classmate of Darby's who lived in the neighborhood and had also recently died unexpectedly. I remember with a smile how Darby had a crush on her in first grade, despite his animated denials to the contrary. The mystery of human connections—how they start, end, and come around again, and in some deep way, never leave.

Although hers was obviously a family in need of healing, Aileen wasn't picking up on Noelle's house, and it didn't really fit the description. But on my walk today, I see that the house with the yard sale is brown, just far enough away to be outside my immediate neighborhood, and I believe that the couple who lives there has been here as long as we have, but know little else about them. Growing up with a sense of social anxiety that has never completely left me, I don't feel comfortable knocking on the door of someone I haven't met, all the more so given the reason for my visit today. So maybe I'll put it off for another day. But my body is telling me, *This is the house Darby was talking about!*

After several seconds of hesitation, standing in the road like an idiot, I decide to bypass my skeptical, critical brain and walk into the yard. Sitting in folding chairs in front of the garage are a large man in jeans with a bemused but welcoming countenance and a pleasant, dark-haired woman. I assume they are the homeowners, and so I strike up a conversation with the woman by telling her how I often walk or drive by and have always admired her irises and daylilies. She introduces herself and explains that she and her husband, Ken, are relatives of the people who live here and have come today to help clear some things out after the death of Ken's cousin, who died three months earlier. Another death in the neighborhood; there is indeed healing needed here.

Business at the yard sale begins to hum, and the two answer questions from the curious passersby examining the potluck of items spread out on the tables. Ken, who has been talking music with a young couple interested in the collection of guitars and amps he has added to the yard's wares, returns to his seat, and I walk over with a smile and hello. He's a charming, funny, knowledgeable man who obviously loves to engage with people, and I take an immediate liking to him. He is what Darby would call *the real deal*, and after I tell him I live right down the road but have never met the couple who live here, Ken tells me a little more about them and why he and his wife are here today.

Ken's cousin had come home from Vietnam decades ago with undiagnosed PTSD and became a virtual recluse. Indeed, while I occasionally see his wife, although not enough to be able to recognize who she is, I have never seen him in all the years I've lived here. He had been a brilliant pianist and managed to make a living from it despite not venturing out of the house, but had never recovered from his war experiences and resulting substance abuse. Ken reveals that he is a psychologist and clinician in the nearby city of Lowell and works with veterans and others with alcohol, heroin, and other chemical addictions. Further, he was instrumental in bringing a man to this area who is actually a friend of ours and also counsels addicts, and was one of the first people to offer support to us when Darby died. My body is in a state of alert, and I see the metaphorical diving board in front of me, waiting for me as I listen to him. As I prepare to leave, I tell Ken that I would like to talk to his cousin's wife, and will come up and knock on her door one of these days soon. But I don't mention my son.

I power walk home, animated and eager to share this encounter with Dan and a little disappointed in myself for my reluctance to dive in and share my own story.

"So, you won't believe who I just met!" I eagerly tell Dan, who is fixing a broken lamp on the kitchen table. I remind him of the session with Aileen, describe Ken's work with substance abuse clients, and what good, authentic people he and his wife seem to be. And Ken is a musician as well. Dan is energized by this news and immediately takes off to our neighbor's house to meet them, chat about the several guitars Ken had thrown into the yard sale, and, of course, tell them about Darby and all the synchronicities that led to our meeting.

"Remember that newspaper article? When everyone first heard the news about Darby and started coming over to pay their respects . . . that *Globe* article the very same week about the wave of heroin deaths in suburbia? How we were so shocked about how cheap and available it is," I say to Dan, now back home. "Ken seems like a kindred spirit in all of this." Dan enthusiastically agrees, and recounts their own conversation and his impressions of this serendipitous meeting and the possibilities of working together for change.

The Darby Doll

A week after Darby's birthday, Aileen and I are on our way to Nashua once again. As I tell her how calming her email conversation with Darby was, she laughs.

"He was pretty harsh with you!"

The *harsh* words sounded exactly like him, delivered with a dollop of his sense of humor and affection. I think about comments some friends and acquaintances have made to me over the past year. "How do you get up in the morning?" "I could never get through something like this." "You're so brave!" Those remarks stopped me cold. I questioned my own sanity: *What's wrong with me? Maybe I should be so defeated that I can't get up in the morning.* I forget in that scary moment when I take all their fears into my body that there is exactly *no* difference between us. Yes, they *could* and *would* make it through. I know; I used to think the same thing. Maybe I used that certainty as a magical shield to let the gods know that, sorry, I will not survive, so don't even try. But, like most, I am surviving, and not because I am brave, but because I am human.

Our conversation turns to Darby's birthday as a barometer for the various ways people in his life have reacted to his passing; some with guilt and blame, some with forgiveness, some not wanting to look at it at all. With his family—cousins, aunts, uncles, grandparents—his leaving has broken the protective, imaginary bubble that surrounded us as an integrated unit. It is still an open wound.

Aileen tells me that her instructions today are simply to walk the pathways within the mall, past the stores and kiosks, observing. Not a lot of people are here, and we follow our stream of consciousness to articulate what is coming into our awareness while we slowly make the rounds. We stop outside the Disney Store, and we share a raised-eyebrow moment.

"Let's go in!" she says with a bemused laugh.

Hmmm . . . "I gotta tell you, Aileen, this is the last place I want to go, except for maybe that smarmy Dead Sea moisturizer guy's kiosk we just passed . . . " I tell her how much Dan and I dislike Disney and the whole corporate fakey-ness it embodies; and Aileen agrees, but also brings into the conversation the concept of our attachments to opinions of such things.

"Did you take Darby to Disney World?"

"Yes."

"Did he like it?"

"Well, yes."

"You are entitled to your opinion, and those perceptions of artificiality are 'correct' as far as they go, but if you dig in too dogmatically, are you perhaps missing out on the larger world surrounding that opinion? Does that opinion also blind you to the life around the edges of your perceptions, such as your son's delight in that moment?"

"Jesus, do you always have to be so reasonable?"

So, we walk on in.

As we amble around the store, the bright colors and playfulness of the merchandise come into focus, and I begin seeing things through a child's eyes. At this point, I tell Aileen how strongly I sense Darby here—he is laughing at the spectacle of his mom mingling with the evil Disney vibe, clearly delighted in what we are doing. Almost at that precise moment, I stop in my tracks. "Look!" I direct her attention down to the floor to the left of us. There, sitting in front of us, are several boxes containing a red-haired, blue-eyed female doll, and on the box is her name: "Darby." The Darby doll, with the tagline, "Think, think, think, Darby!" Incredible! We look at each other and break out into laughter, and I feel my heart relax and take a deep breath. Thinking about Darby, believing in Darby, feeling his continued existence. I remember a dream of Darby as a toddler bringing joy into our lives and jumping on his aunt Joan's back just to delight in her surprise—it's all here! Looking at life through new eyes.

I am caught in time, and he is not. I tell Aileen that Darby is in my mind when I wake up every morning, and that often I catch myself writing the old script—*I can't be happy with Darby gone; not possible, not realistic, not going to happen.* Aileen suggests, because seeing his image I can be fairly sure he is there, that I shout out to him when I get up in the morning, "What are we doing today, Darby?" and do it until I find myself planted in this new territory. It will take practice, but she believes, as I do, that I have long passed the point of no return to my old life.

Transcendent Day at the Beach

We throw a blanket in the back seat of Aileen's car and take off for the little community beach in Forge Village, a few minutes away from her house, for a session in late July. This morning I'm trying to push through stubborn pieces of grief that keep circling around my brain. Aileen understands my almost compulsive need to talk about, around, over, and below a given subject, and helps me steer it in a new direction, one that is solutions oriented rather than repetitive. Eventually, even I get tired of my own hamster cage. Too many repetitions around the wheel, and the tread just wears out.

We walk under the tall pines that circle the tiny beach, stock-still on this hot summer day. Aileen smiles and calls out Darby's name as we walk; she feels his presence strongly here today. I want to. Down at the lake's edge, we set the blankets down, with guidance to simply chat in a normal way, without talking about Darby. Propped up on our elbows, we relax into the slow-moving day, letting the warm sun massage our feet. She looks at me with an amused smile.

"So! What did you do yesterday? Tell me all about it!"

I choke. Nothing. Nothing comes to mind. I start to mumble that it was just a boring day, and as soon as I hear the words tumbling out, I know she's going to bust me. But when I am in this particular self-pitying place, I have to work at even caring what yesterday was about. *Leave me alone, Aileen—walk away if you want to, but I don't give two shits about any of this.*

Instead, I rack my brain for details about "boring" things I would never have even considered talking about.

"Well, I had a flat tire on the way to Trader Joe's."

Aileen immediately responds, "Did you get out and fix it? Did someone else help you? Did you call Dan to fix it?"

That does it; the wall of resistance breaks, and we just laugh at the rigidity of my responses.

"You could see me from the road, trying to pry it off, then kick it, then, the pièce de résistance, climb onto an old box and jump up and down on it! Nothing. Yeah, I finally called Dan."

She continues questioning me as our mutual laughter lets the light in. I feel compelled to go deeper into my story, to question my uncritical assumptions about what even constitutes a story, and begin to see the infinite roads that emanate out through our experience, taken or not taken. The trick, of course, is to look at your entire experience here as an adventure and an opportunity. The deeper issue for me is why I'm often so unwilling or unable to share my experiences with others—to reveal myself. Safety. I feel safe in my sessions with Aileen. The work we do together has a lot to do with digging in the dirt of my past to uncover the psychological mechanisms I created to keep me safe but remained hidden from my awareness. Aileen uses the language of *energy* frequently, and the tools we use to dig with rely on understanding energy as the "stuff" fueling all that is. Thought united with intuition, flowing like a clear river, no strings attached, no resistance.

A shaggy Lassie-like collie catches our attention as it bounces through our conversation on its way to the water's edge. Smiling, we tune into the summer perfection of this day and lay on our backs on the blankets, simply present with sky, sand, and surroundings. Aileen suggests I take a few deep breaths and clear my mind. Look up at the clouds, through the clouds, into vast space and ask for what I want in this moment. No caveats, no restrictions, but be very clear about what I'm asking for.

"Just let it arise; don't question it, allow it in," she says in a soft tone, seemingly far away as I relax into a meditative mood. Even if the contours are not clear, this is how Spirit works. The trick is to be aware and conscious, with intent.

Relaxing deeply into inner quiet, I scan the clouds. I become aware of the warm sand enveloping my skin, the little ones splashing knee-deep in the pond while their watchers chat, the sound of water lapping on shore. Tiny birds, from our perspective, fly high above us, flapping their wings like mad. I breathe deeply, rhythmically. I see Darby up there, and light fills my vision, illuminating in a flash how I am constantly trying to bring him down to Earth, not willing or able to just let him be where he is. I feel the tightness in this motion and in my heart, the desperation and hopelessness, and Darby, who will not come back, no matter what I do. I am tugging hard . . .

Eyes closed, Aileen says, "I see a balloon bobbing up and down in the sky," before I say those very words.

"Yes! That is exactly the image I see!" I see him so clearly, a beautiful, generous presence. Let him be where he is—I can't lose him, because he truly is everywhere.

"Right now, right here, Darby, I release my *need* for you and the life I envisioned for you—and for me." I look over at Aileen; we are still lying on our blankets on the sand. I tell her I feel cleansed, that I feel this truth in my bones today.

We finish this expansive, energy-shifting session back in her office, talking metaphysics. We sit across from each other, and my words are so close to the surface I don't have to dig for them. I feel that another way I may be tying him down in my own mind is by pulling him back into the mask of the ego and personality, back into the duality. Aileen describes an event that happened to her during her spiritual crisis many years ago when "every day was shitty." Absentmindedly watching television at home one afternoon, she spontaneously experienced a perceptual shift that felt as if she were inside the experience rather than simply watching an image projected on the screen, and understood in that moment that three-dimensional physical reality was ultimately illusionary; that what is true in one dimension might not be true in another. And there are seemingly infinite dimensions. Darby's passing is tragic and accidental in this physical dimension and, in a greater arc of meaning, is also the fulfillment of a purpose that has infinite connections and is beyond the human brain's ability to comprehend.

I keep pressing her on whether Darby's *personality*, his "Darby-ness" still exists. She says that Darby heard my question and tells her that I am still afraid of losing him. *That* hits me at my core. Beyond the obvious loss of physical embodiment, the return of his body to the earth, I seem to be uncovering a truth that our bond survives, that *he* survives as consciousness in some way. But it scares me when Aileen says he is everything and everywhere, because, in my humanness, I am interpreting that as meaning his personality, his individuality, is *dead*; gone to me. And maybe it is, in the underlying way I am asking, as what I really long for is my son back on this planet. But Spirit, in whatever way it shows up, is urging me to look further—past that hole in the clouds to the infinite mystery beyond duality.

Frog and Snake

The image of Darby floating above the beach in Westford is a powerful presence in my life right now as I process the emotional experience of pulling him through the layers of consciousness, tugging him back into duality to be with me. Another subtle shift, just enough to allow space in my heart, in my chest, in my vision, to give myself breathing room to be with this reality and to ease suffering's hold on me. Calling a ceasefire to the war within me in this moment and simply letting him *be*, I feel lighter.

A few weeks later, Aileen and I meet again and spend part of our session walking in the woods near her home office. As often happens in our sessions out in nature, we start out in silence, simply observing and noticing what thoughts and emotions arise.

The sounds and scents of high-summer leaves and brush crunching beneath our feet quiet my mind and soul today. I've been thinking a lot since our session on the beach about what resistance actually feels like in my body—the "tied up in knots" sensation—and how to use that as a cue to divert my energy into something more life sustaining.

The strings I held on to when Darby was here on Earth I was able to manipulate into positive messaging: *He'll thank me later.* I never knew where to draw the line between real, healthy guidance and misplaced projection. When Darby was in high school, our church put a call out to young volunteers to visit our sister city in Honduras to help with a building project for a week. I asked Darby if he was interested, as he had participated in social action events in the past, and it might appeal to his compassionate nature and love of adventure. He agreed. The weeks passed, and the time came to prepare, and it finally became painfully obvious that he was anxious and scared and didn't want to go. Yes, he liked the idea, he cared about the project and was not afraid to take risks. But he also was a teenager, grappling with his own anxieties. He saw how important it was *to me* and didn't want to disappoint us. And I was so tied to the *idea* of my son taking on a challenge, much like one that I passed on during my college years—joining the Peace Corps—that I chose not to see him, to turn my head away from what my heart already knew.

I mention some of these mental meanderings to Aileen and open myself to wherever our dialogue takes us. Rather than continuing the conversation on a purely intellectual level, she asks me what images arise when I am experiencing resistance to or release from a thought or assumption. What colors, smells, sounds come up? What memories, fears, joys are triggered?

"Imagine yourself as a little girl walking near a river. Where does this journey take you; who do you see; are you left any gifts?" This takes me back to the metaphorical balloon and Darby tethered to the strings in my hands. There is an irony that in letting go, you don't lose anything real, but in resisting and holding on, you are not free to truly embrace what you are afraid of losing. Paradoxically, letting go creates expansion and holding on creates diminishment. As simple and elemental as that idea is, it is, at least for me, the hardest thing to do. But, that is the gift.

We reach the point in the trail where it veers away from the river and tracks uphill, deeper into wooded areas. It is a warm and exquisitely clear summer day. An energetic border collie, happy to be off his leash, rambles past us after we offer him a few quick pats to the head, his human passing us with a quasi-apologetic smile. We walk slowly, observing our surroundings and whatever else might come up. Looking skyward, I see past the puffy clouds and visualize again the balloon weaving about in the endless blue as I try continually to tug it to Earth to make it fit into a box that just doesn't work anymore. All this brings is pain and suffering. If I let go, just for a few seconds, minutes, what would that feel like? Freedom? I feel the power and beauty in these woods today, and I belong to it. It offers up the message that relinquishing the balloon string will not rip my son from my heart, but put me in right relation to him, to where and what he is now. How do I feel safe in the world? In the course of reclaiming my birthright, my personal power, through this grief journey, I am correcting an ancient lesson I learned when I mistook hiding for safety.

A sudden flash of color and motion reroutes and anchors my attention to what is just in front of us. A frog suddenly hops across our path with unusual coloring, more whitish, almost a rose color, than the two or three we have seen earlier on our walk. We stop for a few seconds to admire it and then pick up our pace again to continue our journey when we hear a high-pitched squealing that stops us cold. We turn toward the noise, look down at the scramble of leaves and exposed root near the side of the path, and see a small, black garter snake with the frog's leg snapped in its mouth. We are both momentarily stunned at this sight and also realize that we've never heard a frog howl! I want to save the frog but hesitate for an instant, wondering whether to "interfere in nature," but Aileen quickly goes over, steps on the snake, freeing the frog who hightails it out of there, as does the snake—no harm done.

We both laugh—the gods can have a ghoulish sense of humor. I tell her I feel for a moment that I have stepped into an illuminated scene from *Aesop's Fables*, materializing to accompany our discussion on resistance and letting go. So I serve up a little side dish of mythological symbolism. Our little black snake represents death and rebirth, a transmutation of consciousness, and the squealing frog is an ancient symbol of cleansing. And there is the human who intervenes. No good, no evil. Frog takes the snake's poison and transmutes it into healing energy. This is its cleansing medicine. We hold on to these deep wounds that keep hurting us, but we have the capacity to integrate and transmute the poison of that hurt and cleanse our souls if we can open our hearts to that possibility. Neat lesson, eh, Aileen?

CHAPTER THIRTEEN

LOVING YOU OUT LOUD
SEPTEMBER–OCTOBER 2009

Hampton Beach, No Judgment

The very first whispers of another autumn blow in, signaling a new season and its signposts to mark without Darby. No back to school this fall, no new apartment, no new growth or direction pointing to the next chapter of his life. But, although my heart is often heavy, I can feel sunlight on the pavement and the possibility of joy and new things. The bones of a new story materialize with crazy new touchstones. I notice a red-tailed hawk flying overhead, this one catching my attention from the many hawks owning the sky on any given day, and I feel Darby's touch as if his arm were around my shoulder. The exact thought, song, question, dream I bring to each session will almost always synchronize with what my teacher brings up before I utter a word. I find teachers everywhere: in random passersby, in nature, in dreams, in parts of myself I never trusted. I nurture trust in the unseen behind the illusion of progress. The crater of Darby's absence fills up with another version of him. Not the one I want, but the one that comes. He just won't be denied.

And so our session-adventures subtly change as my energy shifts into this new space. Darby continues to say, "Hey, Mom, I'm here!" but these field trips take on another dimension as well. Summer heat is not quite over, and Aileen and I are on our way to Hampton Beach, New Hampshire's small-scale version of Atlantic City. This isn't a destination that screams "fun" to me, but today is all about no judgment, openness to all experience, finding joy in any and every day, living with Spirit's guidance, transcending the mind's constraints, feeling love for everyone and everything, laughing with the universe, and trusting—always trusting.

On the coastal road, ocean rippling and glinting before us, we slow down to watch the seabirds from our open windows and smell the baking mixture of heat, salt water, and seaweed as we approach our destination. We pull up and park next to the boardwalk and take stock of the scene. A stroll down Main Street to start the day? The first hit of heat slams us when we open the car doors, and now, we're ready for whatever shows up. Ah, here is the Fun-A-Rama arcade, a place that ordinarily would drive me nuts with the nonstop noise, whirring machines, and crowds of people. But as Hampton is just waking up to the day, there are few people, and the noise is somehow energizing.

I follow Aileen, who can find something to celebrate in almost any situation, into the Fun-A-Rama. Like a stranger in a strange land, I survey the landscape and listen to the game machinery clicking, buzzing, dinging. The place is beginning to fill up, and I hear Aileen's voice from the other end of the building, "Hey, check this out!" Her smile and contagious energy draw me onward to the booth at the back of the hall where she's talking to a young guy behind the counter. She has tuned in to the Darby vibe amid the frenetic energy and asks me if I want to play. I dump my quarters into the pinball machine and win three prizes that remind me of my son—a pink plastic dinosaur, a thumb skateboard, and a kazoo—gifts to bring home for Dan from Darby. Still skating the thin line between loss and presence, although not as chaotic as in the beginning, my emotions fall and rise like a rambling wind; I never know when or what is going to take me in any given moment. A rush of happiness from winning these silly prizes overcomes me, because they conjure images of my son riding his skateboard as a young teen or dragging his big toy dinosaur behind him on the pier in St. Pete on a Florida visit with his grandmother as a young child. A kick of pain because he's not walking this boardwalk, scarfing down fried dough with me today.

Aileen skillfully brings me back to the moment where change is possible. "No judgment, Lyssa. Try to feel only openness and a kind of love for all these people, no matter what their circumstances."

Leaving the arcade, we take our time strolling down Main Street on our way to the beach, inhaling the pungent intermingling of scents: deep-fried food; salty, sticky air; sweat; strong perfume; and some indecipherable fume arising from the wad of gum I just stepped in. This has the effect of putting me "out into the world" where energy in all its forms is moving, in effect, disconnecting my mind from its sentry duty on the lonely outpost of grief.

Finally on the beach, our feet touch sand, and we tiptoe around a now massive array of summer bodies baking on oversized towels, eating and drinking, reading. Some are actually swimming in the cold Atlantic water, but mostly, people are talking, laughing, fighting, and cursing at extreme decibel levels. I find myself laughing out loud at my ridiculous behavior and that of my fellow humans. Will I come back here? Odds are low, but the self-defeating urge to judge is fading fast, at least in this moment. And these moments are having a cumulative impact on my brain circuitry.

I remember that Darby's friend Elise, the author of the video at the heart of the AA medallions story last May, works up here, scooping ice cream for the summer. We search but can't find her, so we get ice cream and say good-bye to the beach. Homeward bound, I begin to integrate the panoply of feelings, images, and thoughts from our adventure as Aileen drives slowly through the crowded streets, noting the synchronicities she perceives. I watch the breaking waves through the open window as we wind our way around the coast, and her words begin to merge with a feeling of calm, as if the ocean's currents have gotten inside me. The rhythm makes it easy for me to acknowledge that I have always noticed these things but rarely felt the courage to own them. We have the universe inside us, and no one and nothing is pulling the strings—it is us in the end, and we have no idea how much power we have to affect our world. This is one of Aileen's greatest gifts to me—she lives her life *out loud*. Our talk turns to the ways of Spirit, of grief, of letting go. A good day will never be what it was—the innocent unknowing of death—but this is a very good day.

Best Corn of the Season

It's early September, and the story unfolding for this session includes a drive into a section of town called Forge Village, past the street where Darby's childhood friend Scott lived and where they spent many days swapping basketball cards and playing soccer. Then down Gilson Road, a route Darby took for a time when he came home late from his job at a new organic fast food restaurant. He seemed to be directing this part of the story, as Aileen didn't know why we were traveling these roads until I mentioned the connection. Now on Route 119, a long, two-lane country road that serves as the only route into Boston for the ever-growing caravan of commuters coming from southern New Hampshire, my mood matches the gray, stagnant sky surrounding us.

Aileen notices Gary's Farmstand's "Best Corn of the Season" sign and stops. Sometimes I wonder how Aileen can stand being with me when I slide into these plodding, dour, noncommunicative psychic spaces. But there is something else, too, that slides in. September always seems to be the real new year, as the growing season and vacation mode give way to reaping the harvest and diving into productivity; so imagining and creating something new is the theme that brings us here. We stop, and I linger outside over the pumpkins, asters, sweet corn, and apples while Aileen has already disappeared through the farm stand doors. I catch up with her and see that she's reading a framed poster hanging near the pies by the front door. It's a touching eulogy to Gary's parents, and right next to it is another, dedicated to his son, who died ten years ago.

Countless times coming into this store—for strawberries, corn, flowers for the garden—and I never noticed or took the time to read it. I tell Aileen the story of his adult son's accidental death and Gary's tears in telling us when we bought our Christmas tree from him that year. And how I'd left the store, thinking I could never survive anything like that. When I say this out loud, she stops me and says, "Darby just said, '*But you did!*'" Sometimes I wonder if this is really survival, but I feel hope in how these words resonate in my heart, and thank Darby for showing up for me, even as my doubting mind continues to push back.

The road is calling, and we pack up the sweet corn and carry the resonance of Gary's poignant tribute for his son as we continue our journey. We drive past the Montessori school, horse stables, apple orchards, and then business parks on our way to Boston—places all well known to me, but today, just a passing scenery. Aileen engages me with the unfolding narrative of this session and messages from Darby, but I feel lost in silence. Yet, talking with her, I begin to draw a connection between my hesitancy to be open with others about this journey with my son and a defining event in my life—the silence surrounding my father's disappearance from the family. I was barely five years old. I still remember with astonishing clarity a nightmare I had soon after he left us. We'd already left Arizona and moved in with my grandparents in Massachusetts. In the dream, a big aqua station wagon with wood panels rips up to the house and then takes off without stopping, leaving a trail of dust in its wake. It's my father. I didn't understand for many years that the man driving the station wagon was my father, but I'm certain now. I had no grownup to tell. Not my mother, despondent and emotionally absent. Not my grandparents, whose bodily expressions left no doubt to a sensitive child that *he* was not to be spoken of. He left, and then my son left.

Aileen suggests that I am dealing with Darby's death and empty-nest syndrome at the same time, so I have been doubly slammed. Events aligned in such a way that I don't have the false comfort of saying that I still need to "be here" for my kid, and therefore put off finding out what my own life is supposed to be about. She says that Darby is now with me 24/7. I ask her if she means that literally, and she says yes without hesitation. But all I can see is that I have lost the most precious thing in my life. What have I gained? Where is safety? Where do I go from here? In what direction? It astounds me how far I can stretch the boundaries of my consciousness and still circle back to this bleak petitioning.

But putting my own word to an old song, *waking up is hard to do.* The continual inner push and pull, daring to imagine new life and then whipsawing back to defeatism, is like a rubber band that eventually loses its elasticity. I am exploring the contours of a new relationship with my son and a new identity at the same time. Little bird's got to fly on her own when the nest can no longer contain her desires.

Loving You Out Loud

Eighteen months have passed since Darby's death. Early on, I felt myself drawn as if by a magnet to a black hole that would surely annihilate me, but it turned out to be the first opening to the light, the first inkling that I had the power to choose life. It was the beginning of a series of choices, or willingness to see through a different perspective.

What if that sense of inner chaos and destruction is simply potentiality, unformed creation—a life force that is an organic, necessary process of growth? How often it has seemed that nothing was moving, that hope was for others, that I walked with a 100-pound weight securely fixed to my back. But now, through a shift in perception, I am miraculously granted a view of life that absolutely astounds me.

These are the thoughts that stir the pot as I drive over to Aileen's on this chilly October morning. I never know what shape a session might take. Bodywork on the massage table? A walk through the wooded trails near her office? Or an adventure out in the world, guided by intuition? Aileen greets me at the door and instead of going up to the office, we head toward the cold, damp swing nestled among the tall trees in her front yard. She has a copy of *The Lexicon: An Unauthorized Guide to Harry Potter Fiction and Related Materials* because, apparently, Darby wants me to start the day laughing. And I do. Aileen and I both enjoy the imaginative breadth of Rowling's created world, but Darby, who had other ideas of what constituted a good read, had taken great delight in busting me for it when he was here on Earth. Thanks, Darb, your laughter manages to percolate upward through my somber mood as fall carries me further into another season of "what could have been."

We pull ourselves off the swing, noticing the brightening sky and what looks to be a fine day for an adventure. Warming up in the car, we head out, this time to the city. I am mostly silent, feeling a rush of sadness, but also a restlessness that doesn't seem to be attached to any outer cause. Driving the back roads to Somerville, Aileen indicates that Darby wants me to listen to a couple of songs she has brought along for me. One was written and sung by some teenage boys from Aileen's church, and it's all about feeling alone—reaching out and feeling nothing but air. For a moment, as I let these lyrics in, I feel

Darby's energy and hear him tell me, "Mom, you're not alone!" *I get it, Universe.*

Earlier this morning, I sat with my cup of coffee before a few minutes of meditation, and a thought bubbled to the surface. That great, existential question about our place in the universe, about our essential human identity as seemingly separate entities in a random universe; is *that* what this is all about—to get that I am not alone? That, in a wider view, we are *never* alone—this is the Big Lesson?

The second song we listen to is a love song written and sung by another young friend of Aileen's that ends with the full-hearted declaration to his girlfriend that he will "love you out loud." My heart tumbles, and I see Darby in my mind's eye as that line filters into my awareness, and Aileen looks over at me with recognition. Even though it happens almost every time, I am still amazed at how the focus of our sessions dovetails, or *synchronizes*, very specifically with what has been cooking within and fizzing in my head—a word, a phrase, or an entire experience.

Just last night Dan and I talked about the experience of sensing our son's presence in our lives and how to talk "out loud" to our friends, family, and even strangers. How do I talk about Darby in ordinary conversation? Not just memories, but as a continued presence in my life that I am admittedly struggling to understand and integrate. Will they shut me down with the silence of skepticism and pity? Of course not. The conflict is all within me as I search for resolution between what my eyes see and what my heart discerns. This is what my restlessness is about. Loving him out loud, like the title of the song we just listened to, strikes a chord now because I'm just beginning to truly accept Darby's absence from the planet. To step out of fear and accept *what is.* Time to "come out" about loving you, Darb.

Aileen suggests that this is a commitment I can make, to honor both Darby and myself. We could all benefit from learning a new language to speak of the ones who've left the planet, to acknowledge and engage Spirit working in our lives.

Dancing with the Garlic Lady

We are in Cambridge now, driving toward Davis Square in Somerville, rolling down Mass. Ave. full of students just beginning their new school year, and it's clear that Aileen doesn't know exactly how to get there. I do, but I virtually never offer to direct people, because I believe myself to be directionally challenged. Aileen pushes me, and when I shake off the triggered childhood insecurity and anxiety—*I will fail; Aileen will be disappointed in me; I will be disappointed in myself; I am never right*—I let go of all that tired shit, and my inner driver takes over as the familiar neighborhoods come into view.

I step out of the car onto a street that is crackling with the energetic quality of a little dust devil. People everywhere. We wander. Darby helps Aileen find a couple of bottles of olive oil from her family's village in Italy in a specialty grocery store we happen upon as we navigate the busy street. For me, simply walking through this city square in the bright, crisp fall sunlight is a joy. There are organic apples to buy at the urban outdoor farmers market; smiles to beam back to the five-year-olds here with their caretakers and flapping their arms like a flock of unhinged birds; the diversity of intermingling ethnicities, cultures, and ages to warm the heart. And dancing through the crowd comes the delightful old garlic lady, an obvious fixture here as evidenced from the reactions, spanning the spectrum of happy hellos to smirking eye rolls. She spreads an exuberant joie de vivre throughout the marketplace with her old-country/hippie explosion of a dress and good-natured hawking, and the heaviness of grief clamping my heart, my lungs, and overworked brain with the opposite of life, lifts perceptively today.

TPP (Time, Patience, and Practice)

Back in the quiet bubble of the car, heading home, I ask Aileen to communicate with Darby for me. Lurking within the vitality I just felt in the streets and social spaces of Somerville is the still-beating heart of a notion I cannot yet let go of—*he should have been here.* The wild, funny, magical juice of the young—*he should be here!* Just like that, I have fallen back into the shadowland where my better angels shapeshift into monsters, waiting for me if I stray too far. And so, too, my continued fears and inner conflicts about Darby's death—could he have made better choices to avert this heartbreak and live out his life with us?

These are questions I have not wanted to ask because they implicate me. I search for Darby and for the bits of myself that remain in the dark. I am discovering a greater arc of meaning to our lives and that love doesn't ever end. But rumbling underneath it all is a vast reservoir of guilt and shame and the absolutely true assertion that yes, he could have made better choices. Whatever skills I had to shepherd him into adulthood weren't enough. I wasn't present enough, or strong enough, or courageous enough. I cannot speak to Dan's relationship with our son; I speak only for myself. My shame and my fear is that he threw his life away and I could have helped him. All of this contradiction has lived inside my head for the past year and a half, and it often feels beyond wearying. *Stop, stop, stop—please just end this!*

I fall into silence in the car, watching the cityscape recede through the rearview mirror for the more expansive green spaces of home. I sense Aileen's energy in the driver's seat beside me, and I want to speak about the array of emotions surging through my body, but I can't seem to muster it. It is midafternoon by now; we are driving west, and the sun is low in the sky, sending its light through the beautiful palette of fall leaves so they appear to be animated with the fire of life even though they are on the verge of leaving the tree. This makes me sad.

She breaks the silence and asks me if there is anything I want to ask Darby, as she feels his strong presence around us, and hears him tell me again how much he loves me. I sit with this for a moment, allowing my emotions to settle, and ask him whether he wanted to come back after he died. *No.* He says he was tired of being in the body, that it was too hard. Aileen interjects from her own perspective that he had wonderful moments of inspired optimism in body, spirit, and mind, but in the end, echoing what Darby just said, it was too hard to quell his loneliness and anxiety, to find the answers he was searching for while contained within a physical body.

He said that my imagining him lying on the ground outside his house on the night of his death, all alone, was projection on my part. He was disoriented, but high, and that's how he left. I struggle with this. I don't like this response. *That's it? You're high; so long?* I feel anger rising for what "he did" to me, to his dad, his family, and friends. Around and around it comes and goes. Is this how the process of illumination works? In this conflicted space of disembodied communication with my son, it occurs to me that the moment of disintegration for me when Darby died was the same moment of integration, when the blinders fell off.

It's been a long day of stretching the boundaries of grief and healing. We are nearing home, driving by the beach in Westford that has been the site of a few key benchmarks in my journey, and I stretch a little bit more. I remark to Aileen that a key component of the shift I experienced here last summer—releasing the balloon that tethered me to a belief that I could hold him here through the power of my grief—is a slow process of letting go of the terrible longing for him and the belief that I couldn't live without him.

As we roll into Aileen's driveway at the end of day, I ask Darby, "What do you want me to do?"

Love yourself!

Just that?

It takes TPP.

He laughs at that one, as does Aileen. Time, patience, and practice. The antidote to falling into that space of mournful absence is loving him out loud. The force of my son's exuberant and loving needling and my own wrestling with time teach me that I am *not* living without him in an essential way, and to live this knowledge "out loud" to the world is a whole new challenge.

———

CHAPTER FOURTEEN

THE POOR GENE
NOVEMBER 2009–FEBRUARY 2010

The Peace Trail

On a sparkling, crisp November morning, Mother Nature calls us outside on this session day for a walk on the Peace Trail near Aileen's house. We enter the wooded path from the cul-de-sac at the end of the road with her two other dogs, Lobo and Alisha, by our side. We don't speak. The air is infused with an earthy mixture of decaying leaves and bog scents. The bare trees watch over us as we pass, and the glorious blue sky asks for our attention, which we gladly give. The dogs have their noses to the ground, and we follow as they take us right at a fork in the path, deeper into the woods and onto tattered bits of boardwalk erected over the swampier parts of the trail.

The farther I walk on, the more I lose that sense of happiness in the *beingness* of the day, and I reach for the words to tell Aileen how I'm feeling, what I'm thinking. For the past two years, everything about my life has been infused with my son's absence. He is everywhere and nowhere, and as his mother, I cannot stop looking for him. But even as I continue to ask the question, *Where is he?* I sense that something has changed. The knot coiled in my solar plexus on the shocking night of his death, both a metaphor for and physical reality of the state of my being, has been slowly unspooling since that day. Now, the coil has relaxed to a degree that I am free to see more clearly.

In that old time frame, I looked for what was lost, going back, retracing my steps—*it must be behind a wall or a door I missed along the way*. Constantly being pulled back into doubt and fear because that inner knot was so big and so tight that I couldn't see. Cycling around this push and pull again and again often seems to be a masochistic and self-indulgent exercise, but really it is just the motion of grief's waves—it will ultimately bring me to dry land where I'm not looking to the past or future for Darby's love, but to a renewed relationship in the present. I know this because I've learned the difference between suffering and pain, and I live in those moments now. But we seem to need to learn these things over and over again until their roots are strong.

Aileen listens as we walk and observe our surroundings and thoughts. There is an elemental fear at work here, I tell her, one that I swallowed whole as a young child vulnerable to my parents' breakup, when I felt my voice silenced. This fear led the little girl to construct an inner sanctuary that kept her still, silent, and waiting; safe from a frightening world *out there*.

My world fell apart, and there was no one to talk to. My father was suddenly gone, my mother emotionally unreachable, my brothers dealing from the same shock in their own ways. I was not validated in that moment. I was not nurtured, not seen. Who could I trust? No one, especially myself. But I had to put my fear somewhere; I still had a life force urging me on like everyone else, and the same Observer watching over me now was surely watching over me then. I looked for places to hide, because I felt unworthy to be seen. As an adult, I did the same; the way I did it just looked different. The child who was painfully shy in school and retreated to her bedroom to ease her anxiety by writing stories became the adult who gave her power away in relationships, jobs, opportunities not taken, so that she wouldn't be called upon to assert her will. It may not have looked that way from the outside—I always had friends, romantic relationships, adventures, and successes—but it's true.

"It was brilliant of you," Aileen responds. "You created a safe space that supported your emerging life through the storm of your childhood. But, as you know yourself, it came at a price—your connection to the world—and it no longer serves your growth. Don't worry! You have come too far now to ever turn back."

"Do you really think so?" I ask, even though I know how right she is.

The dogs have gone off-leash, and we hear them rustling in the leaves ahead. Aileen suggests I use my shamanic and visualization skills to work with the energy around this old story as we continue our walk through the woods. She stops and laughs, and says that Darby is telling me, "Mom, be playful, have fun, love the world in every moment. You are far more capable than you think you are!"

She then prompts me to meet up with the little girl who created that protective shadow world. This girl is lonely and afraid. "Ask Darby to come and hang out with her." I visualize him beside her, and he talks to her in an animated, funny, yet kind way. "How does this make her feel?" asks Aileen. *She feels safe.* "Have her ask him if she can trust him." He laughs and says, of course, implying that it is self-evident. His hand feels warm and trustworthy to her. They go off to have fun together and explore the universe. That's my boy.

Feeling compassion today for my shadow-self elevates my spirit. In this moment, I can envision a life that is open and curious, trusting that I'm where I'm supposed to be. Home seems less a retreat to safety in this scenario than an invitation to just inhabit whatever space I am in. By the end of this exercise in switching up the energy, we have circled back to the beginning of the trail, Alisha and Lobo never at a loss for finding new things to sniff out. As I climb the stairs to the session room, I begin to tell Aileen a dream I had recently that seems connected to our work today.

Sowing Seeds in Dreamland

In the dream, I am involved in the collection of mysterious little seedlings, more implied than seen, late at night in my hometown. I work beside an older woman with short, gray hair—tall, trim, warm, intelligent—who is overseeing a highly secretive, though clearly benign, project involving plants that perhaps have never been seen by the world before. In the still predawn darkness, we set out for several locations, all in my small town, to check on the plants, none of which are actually revealed to me. I then find myself standing outside the building on the corner of Court Street in the center of town. The still steel-gray hour between darkness and dawn is upon us, and the plant lady and I discuss the seedlings. They are doing well and will be ready at a time in the future, probably next spring, she says. Dan appears, walking toward us, and we tell him how things are progressing. The overall feeling of the dreamscape is deep knowledge, mystery, and the transformative potential that will come from whatever these plants hold.

On the night of my dream, Dan was exploring his own dreamland in which our son was visiting him. Dan, gregarious and more likely to share what is on his mind as it occurs, called Darby a bit more often than I did, and he missed that daily communication dearly. He knew in the dream that Darby was in spirit, but he was enjoying doing everyday things with his son, like sorting through boxes of stuff we were keeping for him in the cellar before his planned move to Amherst with his girlfriend the fall before he died. Dan told him how much he missed him and asked him why he couldn't visit more often. Echoing what he told my sister-in-law in a dream last year, Darby indicated that energetically, it was hard for him to travel between worlds. The point was that they were doing things together, just as they had done when he was here, such as helping put up a beam in the new addition to the house or playing music together. Dan woke up feeling enveloped in a warm hug, something I rarely experience in dreams. I envied him.

Are the two dreams connected in some way? Perhaps, for me, it is about the familiar longing for him that welled up as Dan told me about his dream: time spent together doing ordinary things and waking up with a felt imprint of a warm hug. I had an awesome, magical dream, but Dan got Darby.

Aileen observes that the seedlings are my ideas. I am creating something new out of my experience with death, grief, and awakening, through writing and helping to healing others, and I must have patience for these things to manifest. It's part of trusting the process, that Darby hanging out with Dan is the way Dan needs to communicate with Darby, while I have other avenues that serve me better. She also reminds me of the flying dolphins dream not so long after Darby died and their message of ascendance and change in the context of the seedlings' promise.

Before the session ends, we do more energy work, shifting the narrative through meditative, shamanic, and visualization techniques, which I am finding to be some of the most useful and beneficial tools I have acquired through my work with Aileen.

"Work with the seedlings. How would you manifest them?" She guides me to flesh it out, give form to the ideas. "And say it out loud! That's how you give them form and power."

I straighten my spine, center my thoughts and emotions, and tell her, "I want to help people navigate their way through grief and offer the possibility that, although nothing can magically drive suffering and grief away before its due course, your child, your loved one, is not gone, but still available to you through the nurturing of new pathways of communication."

Experiential knowledge, in whatever way you define it for yourself, that there is a larger context in which to understand this reality is truly life changing. It cannot only shift your sorrow, but also change the way you *are* in the world; your perceptions of who you are, how you interact with others, why you are here, and perhaps most of all, what a powerful agent you really are. Dive in, *see it through*, and meet your authentic self on the journey to find your child. Tragedy and grace exist on a continuum.

Aileen observes that I am peeling away another layer of the onion: not needing to have Darby directly involved in every aspect of my life and work. It is, after all, *my* life and *my* work, as it would have been, even had he been here longer. It doesn't mean he is not with me, and I obviously need more work with that idea, because the tears start flowing as she says this. I ask for a message from Darb at the end of the session, as I often do, and he says that he believes in me, before time began and after time ends.

This is who I am on my best days. It's a work in progress and probably always will be. There are awe-inspiring dreams and epiphanies and revelations, and then there is the plodding work and clear-eyed assessment of the "issues"—abandonment, withdrawal of love, lack of safety, poverty consciousness—and the hard-won growth of integration. The work of manifesting the dream seeds never ends.

Stalking the Ocean in Winter

I ride the rolling waves to another turning of the year. Nearly two years now after the walls holding up my old, blinkered life came crashing down, the crack in my perception has spread to reveal a world that exists outside the swampy contractions of deep grief. The bottomless longing for my son, a function of the illusion of radical separation and utter loss, is slowly lifting as I grow to accept both his death and continued presence. While I have been growing tender, new skin, my body has required cycles of heavy sleep and the safety of protected spaces and nurturing friends. But throughout, a new story has been calling me out of my cocoon.

In January, I drive to Aileen's office full of anxiety, guilt, and shame over my financial insecurity. I haven't had a substantial source of income since Darby died, and I'm just frustrated with the pace of my life right now. I arrive to discover another adventure is in store for our session, driven again by Darby, who wants me to experience something specific today. We set off this morning in Aileen's "Magic School Bus," and Ms. Frizzle is ready for me. On the road, bright sun melting the frost on the windshield, we discuss my lack of patience in seeing things through and creating a new, open-ended perspective for my guilt over lifelong scarcity and abandonment issues. For example, do I allow a letter from the bank to be just that: a message informing me of something I can't fix today, or something that will ruin my entire day? I'm either digging the hole deeper or creating space for solutions, an obvious metaphor for the way I choose to orient myself in this world.

She tells me how excited and animated Darby is about the trip we are embarking on, another trip to Hampton Beach, in a new season. After an hour or so, we turn off the highway and snake around the coast, slowly passing by the boarded up summer haunts and the deserted beach and roads, the snow covering what not long ago was a thriving summer scene of sparking life. So here we are in this season of reflection and waiting, what some might call *dead*; the dead of winter. But it is no more forever gone than Darby is. As we leave the car behind and walk on these empty streets, I tell Aileen that what I feel is sadness because of what is gone, but also joy because what's *gone* is really still here, both in potential and energetically here, now. The exact same feeling I have about Darby.

The ocean calls us closer, and we leave the pavement to walk on the windy beach. I allow the cold wind, filtered sunlight, and screeching of the gulls overhead to join the spreading silence that has slipped through my mental gate. I shuffle through hard-packed sand, suddenly feeling so alone—*what am I doing here?* Aileen begins what she sees as a common sense approach in the face of my silence, ending with this exchange as I, slogging, look downward at the resistant beach and she, just walking, notices the whitecaps and seabirds on the winter ocean.

"So, Lyssa, why do you feel you are doomed to be poor, to be lacking?"

Not skipping a beat, I smile and loudly blurt out the most ridiculous thing I can think of: "Because I have the poor gene!" It is one of those moments when the most ancient, cherished lie that I tell myself reveals itself for what it is in light of the obvious absurdity of this statement. We stop dead in our tracks, doubled over in laughter, tears dripping down my cheeks and congealing in the frigid wind.

"So, grab that notion and throw it out to the ocean, and do it with gusto!" she orders. *Yes, Ms. Frizzle.* And so I do.

———

CHAPTER FIFTEEN

Darby Shows Me the Way

have a relationship with the ocean. We talk; mostly, I ask and she answers in her wise and cleansing way. Two months after Aileen and I had our session at Hampton Beach, I want to reflect on where my choices, anchored in faulty, constrictive perceptions of my true nature and abilities have taken me. And then, what a new road ahead might look like when the poor gene goes under the waves for good. I decide to take a solo trip to Nantucket, where the beaches are empty of people and starkly beautiful in this cold season just before spring.

The drive out to the beach from my friend's house where I am staying is a short distance, with only a few other cars out on the road, the summer tourist crush far behind. I nod to a woman trudging up through the dunes, a little terrier tugging her along. Noting the thick layers of scarves and a furry hat almost obscuring her face, I wonder if my clothing choices will prevent me from freezing my ass off. But it doesn't feel that cold to me, and I am soon shuffling through sand next to the shore. I remember Aileen once telling me that when we feel sad or tired, overwhelmed or confused, we need only ask for assistance from the cleansing power of the ocean or the magnificent strength of a mountain. When we feel small, limited, or lacking, we can choose a different reality, the reality of ever-moving energy that shows us we are an active and important part of the flow of all things, including ourselves.

I stand at the ocean's edge, my intention to just listen and allow. I feel the power, vastness, and a kind of hollow roar located within the waves washing ashore and receding. In come the thoughts I brought with me today. If I am letting go of the emotional and energetic strings that tied my son to an old story of who he was, and if I no longer need to see myself as congenitally barred from life's abundance, then the same questions I couldn't answer in my old life stand before me in blazing sunlight now: Who am I? What is my work? What is my purpose? How do I fit into the web of life?

I think of a friend who undertook an initiation ritual as part of a spiritual tradition she followed, describing it like this: In the final ritual, after a series of physical, emotional, and psychological tests, she buried herself almost completely into the "womb of Mother Earth" alone, in darkness, exposed to the elements, to face her primal fears and come out the other side. At the time, I remember thinking to myself, *Um, yeah, I don't think so!* But standing here now, I realize again that I have been going through an initiation of my own, one that landed me at that precipice of terror, and then, to a choice. Follow old programming down the familiar path of lack, constriction, and fear, or intentionally release those patterns and create a new way to engage with my life? In other words, to come out into the light of day, a newborn being. Well, I made my choice, but now what?

I mentally release myself from this ocean meditation and continue to walk on down the deserted beach. I try to stay attuned to the ocean's rhythm and voice, but I'm surprised to feel an upwelling of sadness and tears; loneliness for Darby and worry for his safety, of all things. Just as I feel myself falling again, pleading with Darby to help me out here, a small, pink flip-flop catches my eye. It sticks out of the side of a dune, a lone flower blooming in this cold desert. It makes me smile, imagining the child who might have left it here after a summer of fun at the beach. And then I look down at the bottom of the dune and can just make out a small, gray shape protruding from the windblown sand. I bend down to inspect it more closely, pull it from the sand, and laugh out loud—in my hand is a plastic toy elephant! The winter beach is devoid of traces of human presence, except for a child's sandal and a tiny elephant, a frequent sign I'm learning to just accept as a message from Darby. Thank you, Darby, for letting me know you're here! And thank you, Ocean, for cradling me in your love and power! Yes, I hear you clearly: *This world is your playground, go play with him; he's waiting for you!*

Touching Sound

Nice, mild winter day. I check the floor of the back seat to make sure my hiking boots, usually there waiting for me in case a walk beckons me on any given day, are still there as I approach Aileen's office. On a day like this, I figure a walk is inevitable. But Darby has different plans. He is excited to have Aileen show me a movie and not give anything away in advance. The first thing I mention as I sit and fold my legs under me on the big, blue armchair is how Darby pops into my mind lately at unexpected times, fully visible in my mind's eye and usually bouncing all about. I tell her how different this feels in my body from the images of him I conjured when I was deep in grief. Nothing is for sure, but I am much more willing to sit with this kind of experience and see how it pans out rather than rejecting it out of hand. She agrees this is validation, and that she also always sees him with this bouncy energy—not something she sees with every dead person.

We settle into our chairs and put in the DVD to watch *Touch the Sound*, a documentary about Evelyn Glennie, a Scottish percussionist who understands music the way energy workers understand energy— because she works it the same way. Music, or sound, she says, is not found on the surface of a drum, but deep below, in what you feel through your body. She understands this reality in ways most of us don't, as she has been profoundly deaf since the age of twelve. Music is vibration, energy, and she completely breaks down the barriers we build for ourselves with a simple question to a hearing person:

A hearing person will ask me, "How do you hear that?" Well, I really don't know, but I hear it through my body, through opening myself up. How do you hear it? And they say, "I hear it through the ears." How do you mean that, through the ears? And they can't explain it. And if you can't answer that, why should I be able to?

For Glennie, it is about her absolute commitment to welcome the totality of sounds around her. "I want to be absolutely open to everything that comes my way," she says. This kind of approach opens the door to expanding our perception of phenomena in our world in an altered light, encouraging us to be mentally flexible enough to venture in and see what's there. This kind of commitment to opening oneself to an experience completely resonates with the current path beneath my feet.

Aileen smiles at me. "Seem familiar?" This movie has affected me deeply, and I tell her that it is yet another messenger calling me to break out of the limitations I carry in my mind, to dig deep and feel the energy as it flows: "Touch the sound!" To claim, as Evelyn Glennie does, my beautiful inner core and express it in the things I love most. Additionally, and in sync with my experience with my son, the movie chronicles a visit to Evelyn's childhood home where her brother mentions how close a bond she and their father had, sharing music in the same way. Despite how sad his death was for her, she feels he gave her a gift by allowing her to forge her own life, and this felt like a real kind of power to propel her forward. She carried him inside her. "To learn to use our listening skills, to open up and use our bodies as resonating chambers. We don't just experience *through our ears* after all."

In the beginning, one of my first breakthroughs in the ocean of grief was Aileen's gentle assertion that *we are always safe*. Tears of gratitude and relief on some subterranean strata beyond rational thought flowed through my body when she said this. Why? I can only say that her words found me, and I responded in kind. The shy, sensitive five-year-old who lost her father's presence and mother's attention early in life, who built an inner fortress against the scary, chaotic winds, heard them. Without a strong nurturing foundation, she needed something to hold on to, and that life raft was always illusory. In contrast, this wild, inspirational Scottish woman with a sense of freedom inside her that allows her to travel openly in the world, playing with Japanese drummers in an abandoned warehouse or making music on the streets of New York City with a diverse, multicultural cohort, feels safe in an essential way, because she knows we are all the same, and the vibration of music unites us.

Russian Market

If my perceptual boundaries are stretching after symbolically and energetically tossing my "poor gene" into the Atlantic, a new story is unfolding, with new possibilities, but not without a lot of resistance. I will always miss my boy, and sometimes that old longing winds around my heart and holds on tight, reminding me what a crooked and unexpected journey this is.

It's a windy but warm March morning, and I drive with the window down to feel the first spring breezes brush my face on my way to Aileen's. Nothings clear to me as I drive under the railroad bridge, past the little swamp where a great blue heron sometimes appears, and down her road that looks like all the other roads in this neighborhood. I guess I will see what's up for my session when I get there.

It's going to be a road trip today, but before setting out, we talk about the awards ceremony at UMass that Dan, Aileen, and I had attended a few days earlier. Dan and I received recognition for our work on substance abuse and awareness through the school and the Be the One concert, and Aileen, who had forged connections with the staff at the event, was our guest. When Dan and I were given the award, the presenter mentioned Darby's name in his speech, and tears welled up in my throat and eyes. All I could do was stand there, sad-faced and distracted, as Dan gave a terrific and heartfelt speech, reminding everyone how much the youth—and all of us—looks for and needs authentic, spiritual grounding. It was a call for all of us to wake up to the underlying need for connection and community. After he finished, I struggled to find my voice to convey my conviction that Darby represents all our children and how we need to stop the shame/ blame game if we want true healing. But I didn't. And I wondered why I didn't. I felt hidden within myself, standing there, profoundly disconnected from this gathering of people. And I felt shame that I couldn't speak, for my sad sack appearance, for failing my son.

Sitting at the banquet table after the awards, we all agreed the energy changed the moment Dan gave the wonderful gift of his uplifting remarks to an otherwise lively but statistics-driven ceremony. Aileen added that when Dan was giving his speech, Darby said, "I love you, Dad." But this morning, Darby wants us to visit a Russian market in New Hampshire. Aileen is picking up from Darby that a young man who works there needs us in some way. This is, as she says, putting our intention into action—the intention set in Dan's words at the ceremony to help youth with what they are truly seeking.

The bell jingles as we enter the narrow shop, a slightly cluttered, homey space stocked with Russian staples, including a big barrel of delicious pickles, pastries, dried fish, and tons of candies. The young man is indeed there behind the cash register, and a sweeter appearance I could not ask for. He is Darby's age, and his name is Sasha. Aileen strikes up a conversation with him, and they talk animatedly about the store, the family business, and a car he's restoring, as I wander through the cramped aisles of foods I don't even have a name for. I slowly make my way to the counter and ask him about a birch leaf bundle hanging nearby that catches my eye. Is it decorative, or is it used in some way? It reminds me of the sage used in the sweat lodge, and indeed, he says that in saunas it's used to beat each other in order to open up the pores. "And get out all the family aggression?" I ask, laughing. He grins and tells us it is a family tradition to have a sauna every Saturday, and Aileen comments that this is similar to her tradition of facilitating the sweat lodge.

He remarks on how good he feels after the sauna—clean and refreshed—and Aileen adds that the sweat cleansing makes you feel the same way, and it also has spiritual components to it. Sasha smiles, enjoying what he is hearing, and recalls many Saturdays shared with his family and friends in Russia, and here as well, laughing, telling stories, sometimes fighting, and strengthening their bonds with each other through this ritual. My attention drifts between this lovely conversation and Dan's public comments at the awards ceremony on the yearning for transcendent experience that touches on our authenticity and connectedness. I return to the present moment, and Sasha comments on the fact that he hasn't been to a sauna in several weeks. I like to think that our visit to the family store is like a match, a spark of new light showing him the way back to an emotionally, physically, and spiritually nourishing activity.

We leave the shop with pickles, sweet Russian pastry, and smiles all around. Still, the sadness I carried into the store remains. Driving home, I ask Aileen how loss is transformed, knowing that there is no real endpoint, and she says, "To begin with, you've come to see and experience that Darby is still here, that there really is no death, only a change in form. And then you see that loving and helping another boy, such as this young Russian, is loving Darby. There is no diminishment in this, no losing Darby, because we really are all one in the Divine!"

"I know I've come a long way, Aileen, and I love the idea of helping another young adult, but it just kills me—that old longing wakes up in my core, and all I want is my son here with me—helping another simply deepens the awareness that my son is gone. I feel guilt over this, but it's the truth." Tears are coming on. I don't want them. I feel like a failure; I want to be stronger, further along in my recovery—whatever that means—and less selfish.

The repetitiveness of this cycle of succumbing/bottoming out/ renewal is wearying. And it brings up every negative belief I've ever had about myself, every "failure," every missed opportunity, every lie I've ever told to avoid what I perceived to be an ugly truth about myself. And now I'm being punished for indirectly killing my son with my neglect. Here it is, Aileen; again! But she simply offers me the truth.

"The work you have done is spectacular! Remember the third little pig: build your house from the ground up—it takes time. Remember what Darby said after our Lexington adventure: what you need is time, patience, and practice! Remember, as you have said yourself, that you have lived your whole life from the standpoint of abandonment and loss, feeling that you have nothing to give. But you do know what you have to give; you just don't know its particular shape yet!"

Well, then. I had devised a kind of passive control within my little psychological shelter: I am a powerless agent in the world, and the linchpin that keeps this construct fully fueled and running is the absolute bedrock dictum, albeit an unconscious one, that I am genetically doomed to failure—I inherited the poor gene. So, why bother doing anything when everything is impermanent? Though not the ruling philosophy of my life, this unconscious belief has hindered me. I hadn't fully realized that the beauty of impermanence is the promise inherent in its constantly changing moment. What I lacked as a kid was stability as I moved through frightening, confusing, and life-altering change. Paradoxically, my son's death shattered my reality, and I'm discovering that I have never been, nor could I ever be, broken. It is a transformed perspective that allows for a more authentic connection with the world.

—

CHAPTER SIXTEEN

FORGIVENESS
MARCH–MAY 2010

"The wound is the place where the light enters you."

—Rumi

The Wound

Heroin. I fled you in absolute panic and remorse. No, I never dared come near you in my own young, drug-using years; you scared the shit out of me then, but not like you do now. I needed to know you were safe, Darby, that there is a greater arc of meaning to your death, because *I* couldn't live with what you had done. Because *I* couldn't live with the utter banality of it, with the magnitude of its wastefulness, the unforgiveable guilt of not being present to save you—*to fix this*—that consumed me.

This subterranean river of guilt has carried me through my days since he left. I am coming to life again, renewed from the journey of uncovering my authentic self as my old armor falls away. And yet, there is still something within me that rages that he . . . died? Passed on? Went home? No, he *left me*. And that, in some way, I deserved to be left. This awareness speaks to a guilt much bigger, more inclusive, older. And if I can't dig that up, separate it from who I am and forgive myself, then I will never truly know that Darby is safe—that *I am safe*. Without forgiveness, this powerful insight will simply remain an insight that is strong enough to move me, but will never release me and bring me peace.

Rumbling underground here from the beginning, underneath both my unexpressed anger directed toward Darby and my irrational fear of facing his heroin addiction, is an abiding need to forgive myself for my blindness. Forgiveness, after all, comes from a place of love rather than ego. It's not an act I can perform, but a way to heal myself and open my heart to the world around me. It's a place of personal power. There is simply no way for us to understand how trapped we are within our limited house of thoughts, our own rationality, until the storm outside our door requests our attention, and this time, we open the door. Even then, we get caught again and again. The difference, however, is that we never feel trapped alone for long, because our wound opens us to a greater source of knowledge. It changes us. Rewires the circuits. We don't have to suffer a death to experience transcendence, but there has to be a break with the known world.

The theme of guilt and forgiveness dominates my thinking as May is about to cycle around for the third time, with its triggers of Darby's death day and Mother's Day forever intertwined. I bring it all with me to my session. The clenching motion of deep grief has been unwinding throughout the past two years, allowing for a psychic sweep through the dark places behind rational thought. And I am thankful for this. Even though I don't feel it in this moment, I am still aware that underneath my sadness is an immense well of gratitude for the healing I find here with my mentor and guide, for Dan's care and protection, for the people in my life whose love has lifted me, for the opportunity to be Darby's mother for the time we had here. This is what is changing. Surrender is not something that happens once and is done. My heart is emerging from shadow. I'm growing a new body, and it still hurts.

Reading Energy, Healing Wounds

Aileen tells me a personal story of feeling grounded in truth in the face of a wall of resistance to new ideas and possibility, and how the dead are always around to help—mostly to help us with forgiveness. *I'm not feeling it, Aileen,* I think, but not out loud, because sometimes I just get tired of my own tears.

We lie on the floor and meditate, opening ourselves to whatever breaks through in the deep silence; messages, images, sounds. I hear the words, *relax into your life.* And I think, *Open to life's bounty to explore without prejudice, to follow wherever the evidence takes you; nothing permanent, no finish line.* I've brought a picture of Darby and a birthday card he'd given me. Always guiding me to reach beyond my habit of thinking about my loss, Aileen suggests a different approach.

"Look into Darby's eyes in the photo and tell me what you see in the moment—read his energy. What was he was telling you about himself at that time?"

It's difficult to get beyond my feelings of remorse, but what I read is sadness, love, hidden things, deeply masked pain, and feelings of being lost and lonely. Of course, my own feelings of inadequacy, of failing him, could very well be mixed in with my *seeing,* but the indisputable fact is that after middle school, he rarely smiled in any photo we have seen of him.

Was I the "wonderful mother" he wrote lovingly to in his card? Maybe not a fair question to any mother, but I regret not being more present with him when he was growing up. Did he give me "all his crap" that he notes apologetically? Not really. It was his pain. And I didn't have the skills to be what I consider a wonderful mother: to take charge, set limits, give enough of my love in appropriate ways— because I didn't love myself, and, most importantly, held a rock-solid, subconscious belief that no one, including my son, could really love me. Although we always had a deep bond of love between us, he knew he could hide things from me, because he sensed there were things I didn't want to know.

Aileen suggests I talk to Darby as the mother I could have been had I known then what I have now learned. The strong, capable mother who confronts his pain, calls him out on his lies, even if they are to protect me, and comforts him with compassion and empathy. This is very painful for me. The guilt pot is stirred, the hot tears burn through my closed eyes, and I long for the opportunity to make amends to him in this lifetime, knowing this will never happen. Aileen's help is always offered as an invitation to take a leap around the moon rather than to struggle like the little engine that could. I can stay in my pool of regrets, but the tools I have acquired in working with her offer me another option. Healing can still be achieved and amends made by returning energetically, through shamanic journeying and other techniques, to those events in time with an intention to transform them.

Cleansing the Space Between Us

The road to Amherst calls us again as the second anniversary of my son's death circles around, and we head out on this early May morning with the intention of changing the balance of energy around events connected to Darby's death. I want to move my feelings of guilt and regret, like water, into a bigger pool where they can be absorbed into a greater whole—the mother I could have been for my son is the mother I am now, able to see, able to reach out to others in a new standing place without focusing on all I have lost. Afloat in the big pond, understanding that loss is not a punishment, but a doorway.

Aileen tells me that Darby is directing us to go first to the town offices in Northampton, where Dan and I had to pick up the death certificate on the day of our pilgrimage two years ago. Where doors were slammed in our faces, where we were invisible and disposable, where ignorance and lack of compassion caused us more pain than we should have had to endure on that day. But before entering the building on this new day, Aileen and I spend some time meandering through town, window-shopping and enjoying the vitality and diversity of this lovely college town that has figured prominently throughout the years in both our lives. It serves as a kind of emotional loosening up, allowing for the flow of experience to take us where we are supposed to go.

We head across the street now, dodging cars that don't want to slow down, and I think about how this town has both changed and stayed the same since I wandered through these once gritty streets in the early '70s. Hippie is now "hippie chic," the vibrant LGBT community now key to Northampton's revitalization, businesses growing, the music scene expanding with new venues. It still feels so comfortable and *familiar*. I am happy that I got to share a little of this mutual space through the generations with my son.

We find a narrow side street that takes us back to where we parked, the backside of Northampton that lays hidden to the casual tourist. I take in the mix of old and new buildings next to the municipal offices, one an old "Gas Works" structure, round and made of brick, and completely unnoticed by this grieving wreck who stood stunned outside these doors two years ago. This trip around town has been a tonic; releasing stress, opening up my senses to the world around me, and creating inner space for a more nuanced perspective of how far I have come in the two years since my son's death. Now, it is time to walk back to the Board of Health building.

Inside the small office, we enter a scene of such extraordinary ordinariness that it makes me laugh out loud. The clerk behind the counter looks up and smiles hello to us, and we talk easily in the almost empty space that had given me such pain two years ago.

An occasional citizen passes through for business, and we shoot the breeze with them as well, and I realize that, just as with my trip to Amherst last year for the Be the One concert, there are no ghosts here. For me, the space has been completely cleansed and transformed, and nothing but a sad memory echoes from the walls.

Moving into Forgiveness

Back in the car after a brunch of banana pancakes—perhaps, according to Aileen, tinged with some Darby energy (a prank for sure, as Darby hated bananas)—I direct Aileen to my old landscape, the Southwest towers of the university, where, starting in the fall of 1969, I whole-heartedly immersed myself in an environment that was an exciting, absurd, visionary, and sometimes toxic brew of political protest, open classrooms, hippie culture, and every drug imaginable during my time there. Experimentation and drugs, like my son. There are no straight lines, just crooked ones and mostly unseen.

On this sun-piercing, summery day, we wind our way past the Southwest section of the campus toward the North apartments, new housing for students transitioning between traditional dorms and off-campus living, where Darby lived during his first semester in 2006. As we approach the buildings sitting atop hilly terrain and surrounded by large maples, oaks, and pines, at the point where the road ends, I feel a sharp pang of sadness and longing. Memories squeeze my heart. I remember how excited he was after the struggle to just get here that day, and then, the payoff: the "university experience" of new friendships, exploration, and growth (maybe a bit of romanticized projection on my part.) It all felt good; meeting his new roommates and their parents, helping him unpack and set up, checking out the apartment, taking him out to dinner before heading home; being so happy for him. What I wanted to believe, and it was true as far as it went, was that he was a capable, confident young man who could take care of himself. But he was also a twenty-year-old boy who, despite his admirable independence, still needed reassurance and acknowledgment that separating from the ones who had raised him was a major transition. I'm not sure my hugs for him that day acknowledged that truth.

We circle slowly and mindfully around the dorm on this quiet day after exams, and I try in vain to balance his presence and absence here, on this campus, where we walked the same streets, making friendships, making discoveries, making mistakes. His cousins went here; his uncle and aunt and high school friends, in this gap, this place between childhood and whatever we were to become in the "real world." But my son *ended* here, and my mind simply surrenders to that unanswerable hurt. Aileen assures me that Darby is here with love and support for me, and, back in the car, she begins to channel the energy in a different direction.

She suggests I make amends to him for what I perceive as not being the mother he needed when we left him on his first day. My self-protection instinct had become a shield to ward off disappointment and inevitable rejection by blocking the channel of authentic emotion within myself. So, I don't feel I infused my good-bye hug with an acknowledgment that he might be scared or lonely, and assurance that he would be okay. After all, if I couldn't trust my own authority, how could he? My own lack of love and regard for myself and history of depression impacted his childhood and my ability to *see* him. I couldn't give Darby the degree of safety and honesty he needed. But today, imaginatively projecting myself into that memory, or psychic space, I tell him how much I love him, how proud I am of him, and that whatever life holds for him, I will always be there. And I ask for his forgiveness. The love-bond knows no time or space.

Loss is a doorway—Alice's rabbit hole. It's not a punishment, but a journey. Grief can be transformative. It has as much to do with light as it does with sorrow and has the power to push through stale beliefs to what lies beneath—life forever in motion, inviting us to participate in ways we may have never considered. I don't mind living with my sorrow for Darby, but I don't want to be trapped by my suffering. I don't want to feel like a victim anymore. I am not leaving you, Darby; that would be impossible. But I have to find room for joy in my heart. You are already living there, and maybe I can now release my desperate petitioning for contact. This is what forgiving myself looks like. I ask for your forgiveness and have already forgiven you.

CHAPTER SEVENTEEN

IT'S BEEN A GREAT PRODUCTION, MOM, BUT THE PLAY'S OVER!

JUNE–AUGUST 2010

Resistance and Manifestation

Our session takes us to the small-town beach in Westford again on a bright, early summer morning. But this time, the wind is kicking up, black clouds are rolling in, and the lightning and thunder start shortly after we lay our towels on the sand. When I mention to Aileen that Darby had wanted to be a storm chaser from an early age until he found out math was involved, he identifies this as part of today's theme. She says that Darby is a strong presence today and is about taking risks—expansion rather that contraction—and operating from an attitude of love rather than fear. It's about *being* "be the one."

We pack up shortly after arriving, as the storm intensifies and, as always for these intentionally out-of-the-box sessions, let intuition take us where it will. We head toward the stretch of Westford's historical downtown district, with flags lining both sides of the two-lane street in anticipation of the Fourth of July. Rounding the common as we make our way out of town, we catch colorful flashes of people of all ages strolling, playing, walking their dogs—making the most of New England's short summertime pace. By now, the sun illuminates the last of the raindrops and casts a filtered beam onto a newly opened art gallery housed on the first floor of a small Victorian coming into view. Yes, we'll stop here.

A youthful, spirited energy flows through the splashes of bold color that permeate the space, as well as the young women who greet us, and we are delighted. As the owner tells us her story—how she took a leap of faith away from her degree and the relative security of a graphic design career to create her dream job—I find myself pulling for her to succeed in her artful endeavor. Because she is in love with her gallery adventure, no matter what happens to this brick and mortar operation, I believe her energy will take her where she needs to be. In perfect synchronicity, this brings to mind conversations I had with two friends just the day before.

These friends, both of whom I have known for several years, embody diametrically opposed viewpoints about the risks each confronts. Catching up with Sarah over the phone, each of us at a crossroads in our lives, I noted how often she spoke in the language of constriction, fear, and scarcity, denigrating what she saw as New-Agey, pie-in-the-sky thinking as justification for her self-identified realistic approach. Later in the day, on a whim, I visited Laura, a woman who, like Sarah, is facing a juncture in her life that calls for change she feels she can't ignore. Laura used the language of expansion, possibility, and a follow-your-bliss, heart-based approach. Both were discussing work and making money. Both are facing real risks and uncertain outcomes. And both friends are mirrors to me.

Both are complex, intelligent, interesting people, and I don't mean to reduce them to simple personality traits, but the instructive arc of this day makes me focus on the fundamental difference in how each greets the world. We all have fear. It's in our biology, our genealogy, our cultural inheritance. What matters is whether we harness it to move us forward in our lives or allow it to defeat us. Harnessing fear requires trust. Without trust, fear becomes dysfunctional.

Sarah is fearful of scarcity in all its manifestations. At times, she succumbs to judgmental assessments, self-protective sarcasm, and lack of self-love that affects her comfort in the world. Laura exhibits a strong, forward-thinking sense of self that enables her to say no to her traditional job in the face of unknown and uncertain financial stability and open her photography studio, a long-standing dream. She has plenty of anxiety and yes, *fear*, in birthing this dream, but she doesn't usually use this fear to berate and sabotage herself, even if it does sit over her shoulder, waiting for a fissure so it can sneak in.

That's the difference. Laura is taking a risk and trusting in the universe, because she's not completely hobbled by the fear that stunts the growth of so many of us, myself included. The art gallery Aileen and I just visited is a living example of this kind of trust in the universe. And it *is* important not to get swept up into the superficial, pie-in-the-sky thinking that Sarah mentioned. The outcome could absolutely be losing your shirt on the proposition. But the outcome, the goal achieved or failed, is never what ultimately nourishes our soul, and to see success or failure as verification of the "right" decision is simply not the point. Who knows what losing our house, our business, our lover could bring to us? Who knows what the ultimate game is? It's all part of the play, and it goes on and on. I see myself more in Sarah as the woman I was before my son died, and more in Laura after I have attempted to wake up. But this is by far a done deal. As I am rattling on about all this, Aileen looks over at me while we drive away and says gently, with a smile, "You just don't love yourself enough. That's all." How deep that goes to the heart of my childhood; how far away I stashed myself. I wonder even now how loving myself will ever be possible.

The Ghosts of Childhood

It's a few days past my son's third birthday not on the planet, and in today's session, Aileen wants to focus energy on my heart chakra. My heart is channeling thoughts of balloons, basketball, fireworks, and ice-cream cake. On the fifth of July, Darby's birthday celebrations included a Ben & Jerry's ice-cream cake wherever we could find one on any particular year. Some birthdays were spent on the basketball court, others at arcades, and others on vacations at the beach or in the mountains, where we witnessed spectacular fireworks in different parts of the country. But there is something poignant about that ice-cream cake that brings me close to Darby today.

Aileen guides me back into my childhood to connect with my young self. I relax into the rhythm of my body and breathing and use the by now familiar technique of allowing images, words, and sensory information to arise without the prejudice of my ego-organizing mind, and then work with this to potentially unlock hidden meaning. Aileen is often able to discern the shape of her clients' psychic dramas and can provide expertise on healing, much like a traditional therapist uses her skills to see through a patient's defenses. Today she sees my young self, perhaps four or five years old, near a river or path. I also see my young self clearly, in back of my early childhood home in Arizona, searching for treasures in the gully, the dry streambed where my older brother and his friends played. I visualize myself walking up to her and see that she is totally engaged in her world, collecting mottled rocks that fit perfectly in her small, eager hands; a dusty nickel that catches the light; plastic, forgotten toy soldiers waiting to be melted in the hot sun; remnants of silvery snake skins—objects imbued with desert magic. She is nature-girl energy, dust and desert debris on her knees.

We lived in Arizona for just a few years before my parents' marriage broke up, though not a word was mentioned to us kids, then or ever, about the state of their relationship. We were left to imagine or block out the story between them, each in our own way. This was the '50s, and not so long after Los Alamos and the 1945 detonation of the first atomic bomb, the beginning of the Cold War, the period when schoolchildren were taught that hiding under their desks would provide magical protection from a nuclear war. Of course, words like *Manhattan Project* and *Sputnik*, or the mysterious *bomb shelter* next door, meant little to me as a young child, but my parents were well-read, informed, intelligent people, and I absorbed the drift of their conversations through my body. The anxiety I felt when my mother's face tightened into a mask when my father came home with another shiny new car; when I heard the muffled fights behind closed doors; when my warmhearted dad came into my bedroom to kiss me good-night on the night before he disappeared from my life. And the next day, when my mother fell apart, and I lost her in another way.

Aileen asks me what's coming up now, and I take her to meet my nine-year-old self, hiding out in her bedroom, writing and drawing in her notebook. I lived in a new house by then. When my father left, my grandfather drove from Massachusetts to Phoenix to transport me, my two brothers, and mother back to his and my grandmother's home. I remember him greeting each of us with a sparkling, new silver dollar, which I imagined bestowed magical protective powers. I felt for it in my pocket as comfort on the long ride away from my known world.

Aileen suggests I invite the five-year-old from the Arizona days into the scene with me as well, and I see her bouncing over to her older self, excited to see what she is making. I project myself into the scene, sitting next to them, commenting on her work and trying to coax her out of her shell, while the little girl offers one of her magic rocks from the desert, sensing that her older self needs protection and love.

Growing up in Mom-Mom and Pop-Pop's house, I, as the only girl, was given the gift of my own bedroom in the big Victorian house. Attached to this second-floor bedroom was a small, rickety porch that I was given strict instructions never to use because of its structural hazards. I spent a lot of time out on that porch. Stargazing and daydreaming while cloaked in the green leaves that reached into my perch from the oak tree below, I used my bird's-eye view of the neighborhood to fill my imagination with story ideas. Despite having friends, activities I loved, and doing well in school, I had the unshakable conviction that I was an odd duck—no one else seemed to care about the things that fired my creative juices, and I was ashamed. I was a pretender, a misfit, an alien on this planet, sure I was the only one, and I had no one I felt comfortable talking to. Out here, however, I could let my guard down and find the mental space to roam.

This journey to my past triggers powerful childhood emotions, and with Aileen's guidance, I am able to use the imagery that arises to help clarify what is out of whack for me now and how to resolve it. Like ripples in a pond, psychic space expands, allowing for the possibility of change. I'm energetically "airing out" the rooms in my house, while my younger self moves through each one. She then clasps several thick, cotton shawls around her body, a woolen scarf wrapped around her head for warmth and comfort. This triggers feelings of the tug of generational family history in those protective layers; parents, grandparents, and beyond who handed my brothers and me a "family curse." And the one who *breaks* the curse is the one who wakes up to the fact that there never was one—just heavy silence around what was seen as a shameful secret and who knows how many other secrets kept throughout the generations.

It's time to wrap this session up. The compassion that has arisen for my inner child is helping break down the walls she built that have lingered in my life until this day. Compassion feels like everything in this moment, a gift I have never given myself. It's like a penetrating warmth that melts resistance as if it had been a dream all these years. Tears come to my eyes for the child self's strength, her vulnerability, her brilliance, and her loneliness. There are no villains here—not me, not my mother or father, nor generations before me. It didn't matter that our house of secrets was a house of cards, that it may have been different for my brothers, it just mattered that it became layered onto who I thought I was. But loss is not the only window to the world. I am learning how this works, one storyline from beginning to end. We have the power to change the trajectory and outcome, but only by disempowering the old narrative. This is the native turf of night dreams and sometimes reverie—it is where we go to drink from the well.

Nothing but a Dream

On the massage table, I gradually rise into ordinary consciousness as our session comes to an end. It feels as if I have traveled a far distance, but in time rather than space, moving through a tangle of family dynamics that fastened me to a story of the past and kept me from my power. From across the room, Aileen turns to look at me as she settles into a chair and grabs a book from a small table.

"So, how are you doing? You did some major work today. Eventually, you get sick and tired of being sick and tired," she says with a laugh. "You cannot be responsible for your family."

Before I can answer, she looks up toward the ceiling and informs me that Darby has just popped in and he has something to tell me.

"Mom, it's been a great production, but the play's over!"

Aileen and I both burst out laughing at this brilliant summary. Darby's humor not only lifts the spirit of the afternoon's work a hundred degrees or so, but also enables me to get outside my head, grab a front row seat, and watch the action of all the players in the drama enacted on stage. The family story has a powerful pull and an internal structure that creates its own reality, but it's essentially a script we uncritically accept when we're too young to discern its meaning or choose another way.

"Good things happen to others, not to me," I say to Aileen, a statement so absurd at this point that I half-thought Darby planted it in my brain just to get a rise out of Aileen. Or me.

"Oh, really?" Aileen counters. "How many parents would love to have the communication with their children that you've had with Darby? How many would give anything to have a continued relationship with their children? What a gift he has given you, what an extraordinary collaboration you have!"

I feel a rush of gratitude illuminate the dark spaces. I have watched throughout this journey as each new experience expands my horizon and shifts me away from fear and toward freedom. She's right. I can breathe now; thank you, thank you.

Darby and the Falcon

On our last family vacation together, a year before he died, we'd traveled to Boulder, Colorado, one of our favorite spots in the country. In addition to its stunning geography and high-energy ambience, it's a place that holds a special significance for all of us. My niece, Emily, attended Naropa University, old friends settled there, and, most poignantly, my kind, smart, beautiful step daughter, Wreath, graduated from University of Colorado Boulder, married there, and also passed away there in a car accident that shouldn't have killed her. Her dad lost both of his children. This well runs deep, and the beauty of Boulder retains a special hue for us, both bright and dark.

Dan and I were happily surprised that Darby wanted to come with us, as his life was busy with school, work, and adventures with friends. We created an itinerary that included bits of what each of us wanted: me, white water rafting; Dan, exploring the latest in electronic music with Wreath's husband, Larry, in Denver; Darby, photographing the sights and sounds of downtown Boulder; and high on all our lists was hiking in the Rockies. After celebrating his twenty-second birthday at a sweet outdoor bistro on Pearl Street with an old high school friend of Dan's who lived high in the hills of Golden, I imagined I could just see the beginning blossom of his young adult life light up the space around him.

Darby had recently decided on a photojournalism major at UMass and had spent his second night in Boulder, shooting life in motion on the Pearl Street Mall for a project for one of his courses. He was interested in the emerging field of backpack journalism as a career goal, and to that end, we had given him a new camera the Christmas before. He seemed emotionally stable and animated; happy, healthy, and, if not in love with life, excited by its possibilities. One day, all three of us decided to drive up to the wilderness area not far from our friend Carole's house high above the city of Boulder to climb the trail, one of her favorites.

Endless azure sky and a nice, dry heat enhanced our ascent through mountain rock and fragrant pines. Darby led the way on long, muscular legs, camera strapped around his shoulder, ready for whatever lay before us. We stopped to take our breath—well, *I* stopped to catch my breath, and they humored me—ingesting the sights, sounds, and feel of the topography. We could still see the city far below, with drifting clouds layered above it and specks of birds dipping in and out of our line of vision. There is something about the smell of the Southwest that fills me with a warm sense of equilibrium, so different from the cool, alert sense of harmony of the Northeast, and I was enjoying a silent moment of this when Darby and Dan decided to take off and explore a nearby elevation, a rock formation with interesting angles and a challenging climb.

I began to climb as well, trying to get a toehold, as I heard both of them calling me to look up. A peregrine falcon, sitting on a rock outcrop a few precious feet away from Darby, was staring intently at his face and beginning to squawk. It was an amazing sight, and Darby was mesmerized, taking picture after picture as the falcon's cries grew louder. We were all so enchanted with this close encounter that the thought did not immediately occur that perhaps this magnificent raptor might not want a human eight feet away from its perch. "Darby! I think it's time to come down!" We all got the message simultaneously, and once on the ground, Dan and I laughed, remarking that it looked like Darby had met his totem animal! It was a rare moment.

I think of Darby and his falcon today, almost exactly three years since that vacation moment. There have been many instances of hawk visitations from the beginning—so many that I've learned to discern between "Darby's messenger" and "just another hawk." Power, perception, acute vision—qualities the hawk embodies that I need to nurture in myself to heal. In whatever way the seen and unseen worlds meet, hawk sightings seem to be universally met with a moment of *I see you; thanks for showing up!*

The hawk has become a touchstone for me. This journey with my son has been all about seeing with new eyes, surrendering attachment to stories, and, to all "evidence" to the contrary, to en-*joy* the game of life as it turns through the circles of time. You know—magic! As Darby says, "It's been a great production, Mom, but the play's over!"

CHAPTER EIGHTEEN

Slant of Light

Haddie is ready to break her leash and run with the squirrels, so Aileen and I pick up our pace as we enter the wooded Peace Trail near her house. We talk about where we are right now. It's a week before the Celtic harvest festival of Samhain, the Day of the Dead, when the veil between worlds is thought to thin, and I am weighted with thoughts of life and death as I walk with my guide and friend. I tell her how unmoored I feel lately, unable to remain where I am, yet seemingly incapable of taking the next step. I tell her how, lately, I find myself wanting to run away when my friends talk about their kids.

"Yes, the earth seems to be shaking beneath our feet lately," she replies, as she speaks of her own journey and the challenges arising in this time of unknowing. "The old ways of seeing and being are being released, and we wait in the unknown of what is yet to be created."

Like the changing slant of light as autumn settles in, we feel as if we are navigating new waters, facing old fears, and in need of finding new road signs to guide our way as the energy shifts on the planet. We walk on in a slow, contemplative rhythm, talking quietly at times, breathing in the golden colors, deep-earth scent, and sparse beauty of harvest season. We follow Haddie's path as she kicks up clumps of dry leaves in front of us, and come to a place where the path branches in two directions. I see Aileen make a sudden decision to veer to the left, and as Haddie, now off-leash, disappears from sight, we cross a couple of small wooden bridges built over the spongy ground in front of us. Sudden hints of red catch our eyes as winterberries peek out from fallen leaves and decaying vegetation on either side, and we carefully pick our way through the slick leaves and pungent tree limbs crisscrossing our path. Aileen is ahead of me, her head turned slightly toward a large oak tree to our left, and is about to pass it when she stops short, her eyes fixed on something near the ground. "Wow, this is odd!" she says. Just before catching up to her, I see a shot of brilliant, electric green emerge from the muted colors of the day. It's a cattail, growing at the base of the tree.

It takes us both a second to realize that it couldn't actually be growing here, so far from the rest of the colony standing in the bog ahead. We bend down to inspect it. Our curiosity turns to delight as the lonely cattail stuck into the ground reveals a narrative scene in miniature constructed in the hollow center of an old oak, a kind of ceremonial altar. At the highest level of the mound, I notice what resembles a fort: a shoebox-sized structure made of sticks and twigs, with a doorway clearly cut out in front and a roof of birch bark loosely covering it. A piece of bright-green moss has been placed in front of the doorway, emerging from the tangle of decomposing leaves spread naturally about the site.

Our gaze follows this carefully constructed scene to a space in the tree hollow sloping slightly below the twig fort, where we find yet another element, this one not crafted from natural materials gathered from the surrounding woods. A tiny, gray plastic rifle, its barrel pointed directly at the fort's door opening, catches our attention for a long moment as Haddie's sudden barking echoes in the distance.

Our eyes follow the invisible trail from the gun to a knotted root in the tree hollow where we see a small, bare stick with three prongs set into the mossy ground. And finally, just beyond this at the bottom of the trunk, we find another three-pronged twig planted slightly in the soil. But this one supports a tiny, delicate structure made of an acorn cap and a tightly rolled red maple leaf. It finally dawns on me that what I am seeing is meant to resemble a baby's cradle, or cradleboard. It's a sweet but somehow poignant scene that we've found here. Who created this? Why? Was it meant to be seen by others?

A trail of acorn caps, which seems to be a random spill from the tree at first glance, lines the way from the cradle to the fort, connecting the entire scene. Each element of this diorama slowly reveals itself, emerging subtly from the natural pattern of organic matter in and about the oak tree. Suspending judgment that dismisses it all as unimportant, we find ourselves deeply moved in this moment. Our emotions and awareness perhaps heightened by the tenor of the day and our deep conversation, we both feel a vibration of guilt and war; Vietnam, not Iraq; the death of innocents, and a cry for healing. We can't ever really know the diorama creator's intent, and in a fundamental way, it doesn't matter; offering healing energy to the world is never wasted. We decide to honor our intuition that this is a sacred space.

A Prayer for the Unknown

This is a scene created with much care and tells a story. We feel it is a call for healing, no matter what the circumstances surrounding it. I remember from the religious traditions I studied at divinity school and beyond, and reinforced by Aileen on this day, that indigenous shamans performed many healing rituals without necessarily knowing who the recipient was or what the outcome might be. This feels like such a moment. We decide to find leaves and other materials to surround and comfort the cradle. We gently lay down orange, gold, and red leaves, as well as pine-needle sprigs, and send the unknown recipient healing and love. Aileen remembers the purple asters we had seen at the beginning of our walk and feels that we should go back and gather a few and offer them to the creator of this story, perhaps someone who needs forgiveness. We ask the flowers for their assent as the shamans of old would have done and their descendants still do, and then thank them for their offering.

Back at the oak tree, Aileen steps back, offers a prayer, and I place the little asters around the gun, which she had moved to the side, its barrel now pointing away from the fort. That action stirs something deep within me. It takes me back forty years when my generation's young men were going to war amid protest and societal upheaval. It feels like the energy of a wave that never finds a conclusion, but is the beating heart of life and change. It takes a minute or two to come back to what's in front of me. We look at each other and share a silent moment. Right then, we hear a rustle of leaves and see Haddie dashing out from behind a stand of cattails and swamp maples. Time to return.

Where the Seen and Unseen Worlds Meet

This isn't quite finished. Now, back in Aileen's session room, we engage in some role reversal. On the massage table, I hold her head as she would for craniosacral work on a client. In a quiet, meditative state, feeling a shot of energy from her and allowing images, sounds, and words to arise in consciousness without judgment, I visualize a baby laughing joyously, her head wreathed with daisy petals, almost cartoonish. This baby energy seems liberated and happy, and Aileen asks me to find the man we both sensed as part of the altar in the woods. I see him leaning against, almost *in* the tree, forlorn, with the gun at his side. I feel grief from him; guilt and deep sadness. She suggests I talk to him about my experience with Darby, to offer him healing. He receives it gratefully, and the baby appears in his arms, smiling and laughing. The gun bends and falls from his hands.

I've learned through my studies that throughout the centuries-old practice of shamans throughout the world, it is common in the journeying process to have something gifted to the healer from the spirit beings. Aileen suggests I ask them if there was such a gift for me. An image of the swampy pond near the altar in the woods on the Peace Trail rises to the surface of my mind. I am told to look into the water, and I see my reflection as it ripples and changes with my image and the leaves, trees, and birds that circle the water. This seems to be a place where the seen and the unseen worlds meet. It's a gift of trust and allowing the world to reveal itself.

A few months ago, standing near the French doors, looking out on my backyard on a brilliant autumn day, Darby popped into my mind without prompting, and I heard him say, "I'll see you on the other side!" In that moment, I knew in the center of my being what he meant: that we would be vibrating at the same frequency, beyond the illusions of "sides." Aileen is teaching me what shamanic work is all about, what working with energy really is—that it is a sacred responsibility—and then letting it go. The arc of my experience is widening beyond the desperate task of finding Darby. It's often a struggle to stay awake to this new envisioning of the world, to not drift off to sleep again. Today, I can feel the energy moving. It's an initiation, my spiritual crisis as classic shamanic initiation. She says with a smile, "You're in!"

Wellbriety

Interestingly, the morning after my session with Aileen in the woods, Dan and I discuss the connection between that experience and our interest in creating a ritual object for our family based on the Medicine

Wheel. One of the interests we've always shared, along with music and the great outdoors, is Native American ritual and the spirituality behind it. But we come at it from different experiences.

Dan's childhood played out in an environment unlike mine. Although I always loved nature and being outdoors for as long as possible as a kid, I grew up in a city, where natural spaces were more set apart from human habitation. As a young child, I roved the streets and backyards with a pack of neighborhood kids until dark. And my favorite thing was scrambling up my imagined mountains—literally, a collection of granite boulders in my backyard, separating my house from my next-door neighbors. I spent afternoon hours, pretending to be an adventurer digging up treasures and then hiding them in secret places.

Dan didn't have to imagine wide-open spaces. On his family's 500-acre farm in rural Pennsylvania, he traveled through the fields, hills, streams, and mountains surrounding the farm on his horse after he completed his chores. He traveled almost an hour by bus to school, and his friends were largely cousins who lived nearby, as the population was so sparse. He nurtured a sense of adventure and spirituality rooted in the land and grew up with an intimate knowledge of the natural world through close observation. I took a more artistic, contemplative route, reading about nature, feeling the pull of what I called "philosophy" at the time, but, really, a sense of the spiritual I've had from the beginning. Each route, Dan's and mine, led to an affinity with Native earth-based traditions.

A bit later that morning, I was finishing my morning mug of coffee with a cursory read of headlines from favorite websites and came across this article: "Indians 101: The Wellbriety Medicine Wheel," posted on Daily Kos, by Ojibwa. It was not only about the Medicine Wheel, but it was also specifically focused on a movement called

Wellbriety that employs the Medicine Wheel ritual to heal alcohol and drug abuse among Native youth. It especially appealed to me in its belief that long-term sobriety and change are dependent upon an inclusive community approach. It incorporates traditional Native American rituals, in particular the Medicine Wheel, with traditional 12-step programs used in addiction and recovery groups.

The Wellbriety movement views the Medicine Wheel as a circle of teaching, describing anything growing as a system of circles and cycles, all of which need to be addressed as an integrated whole. The author goes on to describe a ritual for new babies and sanctifying the cradleboard, which immediately brought to mind the miniature structure Aileen and I had just discovered in the woods, with a piece that I perceived to be a baby's cradle. I feel in all this the energy of our broken world: substance abuse, addiction, despair, the terrible cost of oppression, and the lack of love informing our institutions.

Finding the miniature scene in the woods is my story about saying yes to the Mystery and connecting with the world in a more authentic, creative stance. The unfolding of grief over the last two and half years has brought me here, to a new and evolving relationship with my son, a renewed sense of myself, and an expanded way to be in the world. The scene we uncovered in the woods could be a cry for forgiveness, an acting out of hostility, an outlet for a kid with a creative imagination, or nothing more than an afterthought while exploring the forest. But we honor the feelings and energy the scene creates in us. We learn to trust the life force that is within us and give it away freely.

The Darby Drop-in Center

A new story unfolds from the destruction of my old world. Like the ancient, intricate indigenous calendars that characterized human worlds coming into and out of existence, each with its own evolutionary imperative, the new way emerges through a break in the timeline, yet continues ever on. My old narrative was built in large part on the subconscious notion that I was congenitally powerless in the world. When my son died, I recognized, beyond conscious intention, that I had to choose. The death of my former worldview and identity, buried under the ashes and darkness of Darby's absence, or a life in full, calling me out into a world I belonged to? Accepting that challenge has opened my eyes to a world in which, miraculously, my son's life continues.

Accepting that challenge also frees me to give more fully of myself and to define what a healer is in terms of what I have to give. When Aileen and I encountered and enacted our ritual healing at the little "altar" along the wooded path, the experience served to touch my heart and help me understand the value of giving loving energy into the world without expectation, and *it felt good*. It felt new, as if a border had been crossed. And now, I can look back and see that I am standing in a new country. Today, almost three years after my son's death, the pull of grief has lessened, and the desire to live in the world strengthened.

Dan and I, along with our band, Snow Crow, have been invited to be part of the opening of the Darby Drop-in Center at the Lowell House, an organization headed by our friend Ken Powers, who we serendipitously met at the neighborhood yard sale two years ago. We have been working with Ken to get grants for bringing programs into our local high schools to deal with the growing heroin epidemic. Our goal is to create an innovative, workshop-style program that moves away from the failed, "just say no" approach to include parents, teachers, students, and others from the community to facilitate awareness and healing. For our part, Dan and I asked Jesse, Darby's friend who sold him the fatal dose and went to prison for a year, to participate, and he agreed. We envision a creative, honest, safe experience incorporating some of the elements from the Be the One event, with music, art, and storytelling. As a friend said when I told her about this vision, "Well, good luck with that." I laughed but also felt that despite a sure sense of disappointment if it failed, no matter the outcome, a pot has been stirred.

Arriving at the Lowell House in late morning on a misty, warm April day, we join our bandmates hauling our gear into a bare-bones conference room. Staff, community leaders, local politicians, and clients have been invited to the official opening of the Darby Drop-in Center and are beginning to trickle in. Ken once said to me that even though he never met Darby, he feels he knows him. That sense of love and connection is built into the center named after him, which provides a safe, supportive space for people at risk for substance abuse, HIV, and alcohol problems. That mission is a community effort that includes law enforcement and neighborhood organizations to destigmatize and provide services including counseling, needle exchange, and preventative materials for this population. These are people who are not considered patients, but clients who work with the staff in managing their own treatment. And above the center's entrance hangs a framed picture of Darby.

The room is full now, and we are ready to pour music into this space. As I sing, I look out into the audience and make eye contact with a young woman sitting on one of the folding metal chairs that have been brought in for this event. She has her arms crossed, as if hugging herself, her long hair half covering her face. She is smiling, but her eyes tell another story. I am quite sure she is a client, and she seems saturated with sadness, her wrapped arms holding a body that might unravel at any minute. I see Darby there, and I sing to her for just that moment, imagining him strumming his guitar as an offering.

Afterward, Dan and I are asked to speak a few words. I begin to tell our story, Darby's story, and as I continue I see the young woman and the diverse group of people here, and I feel so connected to them that I sneak past my comfort zone and speak from the heart. Tears rise up for a moment, but they are nothing to fear, because I speak from the truth of my soul, and at these times, there is no separation. The truth, as it is said, will set you free. Dan delivers a compelling speech to wind the ceremony up, and the five of us, along with Aileen, decide to walk back to the drop-in center and mingle with the clients.

Mostly, I listen to the conversation flowing around me while sitting at a long table in the center's conference room that is set up for lunch. There are jokes, laughter, questions, and stories as varied as the people who come here for healing, clients and clinicians alike. My focus begins to drift as my body unwinds from this high-energy, emotional day. Time to go home. I look up once more at Darby's picture above the door. It's the same photo we have on the cherrywood table in our living room, nestled among more photos, a collection of elephant figures, special stones, guitar picks, a Red Sox Pez dispenser, and a great blue heron feather connecting it all as if a bridge to and from his life. He is there, he is here, he is in everyone I've met today, alive in my heart because no distance separates us now.

———

CHAPTER NINETEEN

"Mom, nothing has ended—nothing ends."

A Mother's Day Gift

am restless today. I feel it in my bones, in my emotional field, as the anniversary of Darby's death and Mother's Day approach—the annual week of reckoning, whether I want it or not. I know it as it begins its rumbling with an energy of abiding sadness beneath the house I have built. It seems magnified this year because of its number. Five. A parcel of time that the mind can grasp in laying down its history: fives, tens, twenty-fives. Five years gone, five years searching for my son. Nothing ends, but everything changes, and I pace through the yard, pace through the house to keep my mind and body fluid. Five years ago, I entered the fray to find a way to say yes to life, until I could finally let the battle go. And still, out of the blue, a primal longing can pop up, sit with me awhile, and have me wonder, *Why haven't you come home yet?*

The Facebook messages from his friends and family have started coming in to the Darby memorial group page, but I'm not ready for that. I have competing desires to either write a soulful meditation on this five-year marker or disappear into silence for a while. I am running today, but whether to or from something, I'm not sure. I dart up to my office in late afternoon, just long enough to boot up my laptop and then return to the kitchen to talk to Dan about my mixed emotions and see how the day is presenting itself to him. A short time later, I open the door to the new addition to our house, where I have my office. As I climb the stairs, I hear a faint sound from behind the office door—music, getting louder as I approach. What *is* that? I hadn't opened iTunes or anything else on my computer before I went down to talk to Dan, so it's a mystery. I walk in, and to my amazement, "Alive in This World" is blaring from the MP3 on the desktop. I hadn't clicked it, but there it was, the very song I often turn to when missing Darby, written by our friend Neal Ward after Darby's memorial. The song is not so much a meditation on death as it is an uplifting call to connection, creativity, and joy in the face of human frailty, at the very heart of life here on Earth. It's the song that most connected me to Darby in the beginning days and never failed to massage my heart.

I feel such an uprising of happiness, after the unease of the day, that I simply stand there, thanking Darby, as well as Neal for the gift of his song. It doesn't matter at all how this came to be; Darby is clearly telling me, with no distance between what I believe and what I know, that he is here, *alive in this world*, and I rejoice. It slowly dawns on me that it was roughly this time of day five years ago that he had called out of the blue to simply shoot the breeze with me and happened to catch both Dan and his grandmother at the house as well. It was our last conversation. I take in this amazing thread of communication weaving through the past five years: wanting it, resisting it, learning its ways. I feel very loved in this moment.

Gratitude, forgiveness, trust. When did I cross that sublime borderline? Each one of these postures is a portal to expansion to a bigger life than I could have imagined or perceived. And the golden key to this kingdom is total surrender. How did I know that? It's a mystery, it was an act of grace, and it opened all the doors and continues to do so. From this vantage point, five years after my son's death, I can fully embrace the truth that surrendering is not a passive stance of resignation, rather the doorway to authentic experience. You have to go quiet to hear it and talk to it. You have to be willing to face your fear and stand up to its minions at the gate: cynicism, self-abasement, judgment—all these things that keep us blind and needy. Five years ago, the proposition that I could feel any kind of gratitude or forgiveness, or most of all, trust in the *what is* of life, was incomprehensible. I did not have the eyes to see or the ears to hear, yet I see that this hidden path I chose was the only way for me. A journey I was too blown away to think about, otherwise I might never have taken it.

I remember a time in the late '80s when I had just returned to school to finish my BA, with a husband doing the same, a toddler in daycare, and going through tremendous change in our lives. I'd come home and watched *The Power of Myth* on PBS, enthralled by the conversations between Bill Moyers and Joseph Campbell: the beauty and power of the ancient myths, universal and timeless, as Campbell took his viewers to the realm of archetype and story with roots deep in human consciousness. He spoke of the hero's journey, the "hero with a thousand faces"—the shaman's initiation in indigenous cultures—in which the initiate must undergo a cycle of trauma, tests of courage, unconditional trust, and loss of everything s/he thought s/he was, and, finally, transcendence and transformation. What I didn't know then is that everyone has that hero and that initiation within, whether they take it or not. It humbles me.

White Roses

Having nurtured a dim view of the commercialization of Mother's Day over the years, I was nonetheless happy enough to throw that view overboard when my own kid drove down from Amherst with a giant wheel of brie and bottle of wine from his after-school job at Whole Foods. But this journey has taken me to the heart of another aspect of Mother's Day, one that comes around every May with its own significance and curious synchronicity. Dreams in the first few months after Darby died came in searing fragments or full-blown symbolic storylines too painful to think about, much less write down. One of them, however, had special significance and recurred several times over the next five years. I dreamed of white roses just after his death, near Mother's Day in 2008.

Night has come. Darby is lying stretched out in the backseat of a car, his dad driving (although we seem to be stationary) as I clutch my seat on the passenger side. Darby holds a bouquet of white roses in his arms and is weak and very sick. He doesn't say anything; he can't. I look back at him and have a desperate thought that if he can just stay in the backseat until sunrise the next day, he will stay alive. Fade out, wake up, bury it deep.

This buried dream was planted like a seed that spring. I remembered it the next Mother's Day, because the dream had something to say to me—I was sure of it. It had taken me a full year to find the space in my mind and heart to allow the images to unfold and stay long enough for me to feel my way through them. I could still feel the panic and enormity of what was happening as I allowed the dream images in. No wonder I'd buried it—my boy seemed to be slipping away from me, and there was nothing I could do about it except hope for a miracle I knew in my gut would never come. Most heartbreaking of all was the bouquet of white roses, cradled in his weakening arms, that seemed to be a gift of love—his love for me—that was leaving this world. I was a year past his death then, and struck by the symbolism of this dream, and I looked into literature and myth for meaning.

White roses can point to otherworldliness and love that is stronger than death. Does the element of survival at sunrise in my dream point to resurrection in some sense? In Greek myth, Orpheus, playing his lyre down through the underworld, tries to bring his wife, Eurydice, who had been bitten by a snake and died in the flower of her youth, back to the land of the living. But he slipped up and broke the one condition set for him: *Don't look back* until once again in the safety of the upper world. She was lost to him forever. Like pieces of a jigsaw puzzle, I held the dream images in my hand but couldn't quite fit them together.

I carried the thread of the white roses dream with me to Aileen's healing room on a cold November day, four and half years after it first visited me. I described the dream and how painful it was, too painful to write down at the time of his death, but how it surfaced almost every year in the spring or fall, as it had yet again. She asked me to draw the energy of sorrow. I painted a scene of nighttime: orange moon looking down, observing, mirrored within the deep blue of a lake below. It evoked clarity and depth of feeling, not the confusion and despair of gray clouds and barren landscape. I knew then, yet again, that the sorrow I felt affirmed my connection with Darby, but my suffering only separated us.

As she worked with energy blockages in my body on the massage table, I describe the dream: My mind's eye rests on my son, gravely ill, his gift of roses a sad good-bye. My mind accepts this image at face value and tries to make meaning of it. What was Darby telling me? Seeing him lying there was so sad, it made me cry. But Aileen changed up the energy and guided me to look at this scene from a different angle, in a different light. Who or what was in the backseat?

"Not with your mind, but with your emotions. Stay with it . . ."

Yes . . . it's me—I *am lying in the backseat!* I see it immediately when I let my mental guard down and allow the emotional water carrying the dream images into my imagination. Darby's body—its frailty, the almost-fetal position, his sorrowing countenance—encompassed the entirety of my desperation and guilt, my utter powerlessness to save my son. Because, of course, Darby was free, flying over Acadia. This is my own "resurrection," my own transformation.

The truth of Darby is in the roses—the light for my awakening. This is my journey through grief, healing, and transformation, the gift of life he was able to give me because *he* has life—he *is* Life. *He* is the gift. This is no sacrifice, but a gift. No need to look any further for meaning than that. As the session came to an end, Aileen said Darby is there, standing behind me observing. "You did it," she said. "You came through it and survived."

Tonight, sitting in my office before going down to have supper with Dan, the breakthrough truth of that session last fall brings tears to my eyes, not because of grief but for gratitude for my boy and the precious years we had with him, and the life I get to live here on Earth. He is *alive in this world* in an elemental way I can't fully explain or possibly deny. He affirmed it today when I needed it the most, calling me up the stairs to hear the song he knew would open me up. I click on iTunes and play it once more. Half-listening, half-feeling the music as the background and setting for this day, I catch lyrics as they come by: images evoking the joy of sharing our stories, the echoes of everyone who has lived on this Earth, the celebration of a life that is alive in everyone you touched.

Alive in This World

Aileen once asked me how, as a lover of nature, I *know* the things I see in the natural world. After a long pause, I finally told her that I felt their essence alive in my body. I feel Darby the same way—this is what I know. What it ultimately means in the grand scheme of the mysterious universe, I can't say.

Red-tailed hawks, great blue herons, a toy elephant sticking out of the sand on a deserted beach, sobriety medallions manifesting at the benefit concert, a double rainbow appearing out the window of a Scottish inn just as we were celebrating your birthday. I don't know anyone who has not had magical, sometimes inexplicable experiences like these. Messages sent from ones we love who are no longer embodied on Earth—this is how I interpret them. The wildness, beauty, and destructive force of nature is in us, and it is, as far as I know, beyond our ability to fully comprehend.

On a long-ago vacation on Mount Desert Island at Acadia National Park in Maine when you were seven or eight years old, we were scrambling over the rocks and stunted brush on the stunning rock face above the ocean. Dad and I found a place to sit among the boulders and blue sky, and you skipped ahead, a little farther down the cliff to inspect what the sea had left with the ebbing tide. Peaceful, expansive—what better place on Earth to be at this moment? Laughter and muffled voices echoed from different directions all along the cliff, and Dan walked over toward the voices to join the rest of the family. I looked down to where you were, just a short distance from the place I rested, legs outstretched and hiking boots perched clumsily across the granite shelf, the sun warming my bones, and then I saw it. A wave came roaring over the rocks and receded so quickly and so close to you that it took a few seconds to register; a horrified realization that the wave could have taken you with it.

I was speechless. I rushed down to you, and you were busy investigating the tide pools, oblivious to the scene I witnessed. I was relieved beyond measure that you were okay, wondering how I could have left you there, how I could have not imagined the danger. But to you, it's as if nothing happened—and indeed, nothing had—and you came back up the trail with your treasures, and we all munched on our sandwiches and apples together. Everything happened in that moment. I saw your death in that moment, although I pushed it back out to the rolling ocean as soon as the horror began its ascent in my awareness. I embraced your life and the "simple twist of fate" that flipped the coin in that moment.

Years before that, we celebrated Darby's birthday just hours after a young man drowned in Horsethief Lake below our South Dakotan campground. When we heard the screams from afar, those of us camping there had rushed to find help from the park rangers, but it was too late. Late that night, feeling restless, I got up and stepped outside the tent when everyone had gone to bed. The wind had picked up, and the clouds swirled with tremendous energy through the night sky. I shivered despite the summer heat and remember feeling as if the sky had closed up over a gaping hole that had erupted around that young man slipping under the water. And then, just an eerie, thundering silence. What I know is that a powerful force of nature whirled through a great silence, and it got inside me, like the spinning sky that night out on my steps a week after Darby died.

———

This morning, thirteen years to the day after our son left the planet, Dan and I sip our coffee and look out over our big backyard with spring greening everything in sight. The incongruity of Darby's— and his sister, Wreath's—death day coinciding with this most gentle and blossoming month, although diffused over the years, has always jolted me.

I think back to that charged night a few days after Darby died and the preternatural calm that blanketed me while I sat, stunned, on the front steps. I reflect on the questions I asked and the long, spiraling road taken to answer them. There would be no *moving on*; instead, a diving into the center of the storm with eyes open. None of it is what I thought it would be. All of it required new frameworks of understanding. I found him because he never left. The motion I rode was like a lightning bolt that took me deeper and deeper into the Mystery rather than away from it. The healing I found wrapped itself around a scar so deep I can't imagine my life without it. I have learned to love it and honor it. My son's death didn't break me. It didn't diminish me or condemn me to a lesser life. It broke me open, and I found him there, in the space between.

These days, there are more moments of no-separation than not, and in those moments, I feel the end of grief, with only sadness remaining. And I will always miss him. Sadness will always find me when I think of what might have been, when I would give anything to look into his eyes and hug him. *And* he is with me always. The light of love is indestructible, and the other side of profound grief is pure joy. I have experienced that, too. This is the bargain we make with the Mystery, both integration and the paradox of life here on Earth.

Every Wednesday, I'd show up at Aileen's door, heart and mind open to whatever the universe had in store for us. And by universe, I mean my son. Our entire time together has been about Darby's art, his expression, what he wanted us to see. Everything he showed us was his artwork, his orchestration: "Mom, it was the colors from the crayon box I chose!" Aileen was the energy tracker and tour guide, translating for me. And I was the seeker, on a mission to find my boy. He brought us into his world, which is *our* world; we just can't see it.

What I believe is that there is no afterlife, just this life, with no beginning and no end, revealing itself as we grow eyes to see it. This is Darby's life, death, and transition. This is my destruction, transformation, and rise from the ashes. All of us—alive in this world.

———

Acknowledgments

Walking through grief may be a lonely enterprise, but the love, support, and simple presence given freely are the things that carry us home. My deep gratitude to all those who offered us a word, a hug, a book, a walk in the woods, a home-cooked meal, and so many more acts of kindness.

Love and thanks to my family: my husband, Dan, partner on this path. To my brothers, Dana, Christian, Jeff, Robin, and sister-in-law, Joan. To my nieces and nephews, Heather, Johanna, Emily, Eric, and Mark. To my mother, Jane, and mother-in-law, Violet Gowland.

To my friends and bandmates, Bev Rodrigues, Andy Sadler, Steve Campbell, Tim Langevin, and Ross Lama, with thanks to Bev for her close and insightful reading of the early manuscript.

My writers group: Molly Salans, Catherine Gregory, Elizabeth Selders, Ellen Todd, and Katharyn Dawson.

To my editor, Parthenia Hicks, whose sharp and empathetic eye made this a better book.

To my spiritual community: Aileen Dashurova, Laurie Thibault, Nora Buckley, Martha Oesch, Ken Flanders, Sharon Horen.

Love to Darby's friends and to our First Parish Church of Groton, MA community, who buoyed us through those first days.

To my dear friend, mentor, and co-conspirator Aileen Dashurova. And a special thanks to our friend Neal Ward whose beautiful song, "Alive In This World," inspired the title of this book.

ABOUT
LYSSA BLACK FASSETT

Lyssa Black Fassett is a writer, musician, former researcher, and lover of the natural world. She has had a lifelong interest in spiritual, religious, and philosophical thought, experimenting with various practices such as insight meditation, shamanic journeying, and goddess traditions, eventually leading to a master's degree at Harvard Divinity School. But none of this remotely prepared her for the sudden death of her 22-year-old son from a heroin overdose. Her story details a kind of "archaeological dig" of a transformation born of traumatic grief, years of struggle and grace, a perceptual shift pointing the way home to herself, and to an altered, yet unbroken, relationship with her son. Lyssa lives with her husband in a small town northwest of Boston, where they raised their child.